Party!

SIMPLE AND DELICIOUS PARTY FOOD

Party!

SIMPLE AND DELICIOUS PARTY FOOD

Love Food ™ is an imprint of Parragon Books Ltd

Parragon
Queen Street House
4 Queen Street
Bath BA1 1HE, UK

Copyright © Parragon Books Ltd 2007

Love Food ™ and the accompanying heart device is a trademark of Parragon Books Ltd.

Photography by Mike Cooper
Additional photography by Don Last
Design by Talking Design
Introduction text by Frances Eanes
Additional recipes by Beverly Le Blanc

PICTURE ACKNOWLEDGEMENTS
Love Food ™ would like to thank Corbis for permission to reproduce copyright material on pages 9, 14, 36, 60, 84, 106, 130, 154, 176 and 200.

ISBN: 978-1-4075-0117-8

Printed in China

NOTES FOR THE READER
This book uses imperial, metric, and U.S. cup measurements. Follow the same units of measurement throughout; do not mix imperial and metric. All spoon measurements are level, unless otherwise stated: teaspoons are assumed to be 5 ml and tablespoons are assumed to be 15 ml. Unless otherwise stated, milk is assumed to be whole, eggs and individual fruits, such as bananas, are medium, and pepper is freshly ground black pepper.

Recipes using raw or very lightly cooked eggs should be avoided by infants, the elderly, pregnant women, convalescents, and anyone suffering from an illness. Pregnant and breast-feeding women are advised to avoid eating peanuts and foods containing peanuts.

Contents

Introduction

The perfect party should be stylish and quietly sophisticated, with a chic atmosphere and suitable food and drink. A party should be something out of the ordinary and, if well-planned, will inspire those you invite to look the part and appreciate your flair for faultless socializing. This is not about throwing a party-hat-and-games gathering; this is selective, invitation-only entertaining.

Everyone who hosts a party should feel the warm glow that comes with knowing they've thrown the hit of the season and that their guests will leave happy and excited about the next gathering. The secret to entertaining is calm organization and a taste for the finer things in life. Parties are flexible affairs, from birthdays, cocktail parties, and Mardi Gras celebrations, to spa parties, garden parties, and brunch gatherings. In fact, why do you even need an occasion? Why not throw a party just because you can? It's a wonderful way to celebrate the things you love—laughter, best friends, and family; showing off a gorgeous new pair of shoes; eating delicious food and enjoying divine wine or naughty cocktails—there you have several good reasons for a perfect party! It really is as easy as that.

This book is packed with practical advice, recipes, drinks, menus, and more, to help your party become the hottest event on the scene. Hosting a party provides the opportunity to try certain new things; for example, if you want to attend a fancy cocktail soirée so you can wear that dress you've been saving, then why not host it yourself? Once you've organized one and seen how easy and enjoyable it is, you'll be planning the next occasion even before your guests leave.

The Essential Details

• Warn your nearest neighbors. Any party organizer will tell you that it's only polite to mention that you're having a gathering; bear in mind parking problems, too.

• Don't forget, before setting a date, to coordinate calendars with key guests. Remember that most people have a packed social schedule and there is no point in planning a party for an evening when everyone has a prior engagement, especially around busy times like Christmas and Easter.

- Seek help in putting together the perfect party. For example, look into the possibility of hiring flatware or silverware. There are establishments that will even collect all the used equipment the following day so you can cut back on the cleaning-up operation!

Invitations

- Invitations are crucial in setting the tone for an event. Preparing your invitations—whether bought or made—will raise excitement and allow you to set the scene for your gathering.

- Important information includes the venue, date, time, and occasion for the party. Ask invitees to reply (RSVP) by a certain date and if you are encouraging a "plus one" allowance, then say so. It's also worth asking guests to mention any food preferences they may have.

- For large parties, save yourself some work and buy the invitations. Try looking in small art galleries or boutiques to find unusual and elegant designs.

- For a smaller number of guests you may want to design your own. You could hold a pre-party creative evening with a couple of arty friends to get the ideas rolling. Think minimal, tailored designs and you can't go wrong.

- First impressions are always important, so why not hire a smart-looking, butler-type gentleman to tend the door for your party? Give him a guest list to check off. This is sure to set up an evening of style and sophistication!

Food

- Planning the menu is crucial to the art of throwing a good party. People will always remember the food, so make sure you have a rough idea of quantities as there is nothing worse than bare platters and hungry guests!

- How you serve the food should reflect what sort of party you are holding. Buffet food can be chic and relaxed and encourages people to mingle and chat; if you are hosting an intimate gathering of old friends or close family, then a brunch or barbecue party may be perfect.

- Although food is crucial, it is better to master straightforward dishes with style than try an overcomplicated and fussy menu that may go wrong.

• Make sure that guests can dispose of toothpicks or used table napkins easily by placing baskets strategically around the room.

• Remember, parties are supposed to be fun for the host too, so plan the food, execute with panache, and then spend the actual party socializing with your guests.

Drink

• It is better to supply too much than too little in the drinks department. Good party etiquette means that guests will probably bring a bottle or two, although this is not usually the case for more sophisticated occasions.

• Shopping online is a great way to avoid carrying heavy boxes, but don't buy too much hard liquor; keep it simple and uncomplicated. Unless you're specifically hosting a cocktail party (page 84), stick to wine and beer, with a few classics such as vodka, bourbon, rye, and scotch.

• You can jazz up the drinks with a seductive selection of mixers—cranberry juice, orange juice, and tonic water— and some juicy, fresh trimmings, such as limes, cherries, olives, and orange and lemon slices.

• Don't forget plenty of non-alcoholic alternatives. If you want to be creative, you can offer a Bubbly Peach & Mint Tea Punch (page 57).

• Offer good-quality domestic sparkling wine if you can't afford a good champagne. There are some excellent California and Oregon vintages.

• Always make sure that you have enough of the correct style of glasses for a variety of drinks. There is nothing worse than showing up for a party in a stylish dress and high heels, only to have to drink a Cosmopolitan from a beer mug!

The Tableware

• Tableware is something that guests may not consciously notice, but it will add to the overall impression of elegance if done well.

• Pick your table linen carefully—go with clean designs and minimal colors and steer clear of bold prints (unless they are tasteful). If you can, try matching your table to the theme of your party; for example, for a cocktail party try dark plain linen, edged with gold for a striking effect. For a Mardi Gras party think about bright colors and bold exotic flower arrangements. If you are holding a spa party, your color scheme should be calmer, highlighting soft pastel shades.

• It is also important to think about sufficient flatware, silverware, and serving utensils, that can be hired or borrowed from friends. If you can, try to make sure that worn, ill-matching serving utensils don't spoil the fabulous spread of food and careful table dressing.

• Napkins are crucial for finger food. If you forget this

detail and have to resort to paper towels on the night, this could spoil much of the ambience you've created! For an extra touch, try folding napkins simply, at bold angles, and arranging them 5–10 per plate for the buffet table, spread like a fan of playing cards.

• Try to theme the table decorations. For a garden party celebration, float individual flower heads (orchids are stunning) in a matching collection of short, thick-cut glass vases. For a spa party, simple pebble arrangements or even a small water feature (available from most hardware stores) placed on a side table will create the perfect environment for relaxed entertaining.

• Should you need extra help, don't be afraid to hire professionals. This will leave you free from worry and add a certain something if you ask for the staff to look neat and well presented.

Decor

• There are a few simple things you can do to transform your home into the perfect party venue. First, clean and clear away any valuable or breakable items that may be in the way.

• Remove or reposition chairs, leaving only a few, so that people circulate and don't stay glued to their seats.

• Lighting is crucial, depending on your theme. It should

be soft and seductive without being murky and dark. Candles are always perfect and small Christmas lights can provide an atmospheric glow. For a garden party, Chinese-style lanterns, luminarios, and elegant candles mean you can keep on partying long after dark.

• Music plays an essential part in creating the right mood. You could prepare a compilation of appropriate music—soft jazz for a cocktail party or more lively music for a Mardi Gras party to encourage chatter and maybe some dancing later in the evening! If you are holding a brunch party, why not ask people to bring their own favorite lazy-day tunes. For your spa party it's worth purchasing a collection of meditation music. Don't have the music at too high a volume, as people want to talk, and not shout over it.

• Clean the bathroom, remove all personal belongings, add

some high-quality soap and hand cream, provide paper or cloth hand towels, and a wicker basket for any waste.

- Flowers in the main room, hallways, and bathroom really change the emphasis from ordinary to exceptional. Again, try to theme the arrangements and be inventive. For a Mardi Gras party, you could try an arrangement of palm leaves interspersed with a few gorgeous bird-of-paradise blooms.

- You can protect furniture by using Scotchgard, and it may be worth rolling up valued rugs and storing them in another room.

- Put out plenty of coasters to protect furniture—tables and buffets.

- You will need to provide an area for leaving coats, either a closet or bedroom. Depending on the size and type of party, think about removing any pets (shut them in a separate area or put them in "kennels" for the day). It may be a good idea to arrange for children to sleep over with friends for the night.

- The temperature of the main party room needs to be comfortable. In the winter, make sure the heating has been on to welcome guests and keep them warm later. In the summer, think about adding electric fans or a freestanding air-conditioning unit, to prevent people from feeling too hot and bothered.

- You need to decide whether yours will be a smoking inside or outside party. If inside, supply plenty of ashtrays. If outside, set aside a patio area with a table dressed with candles, ashtrays, and maybe a few nibbles. Take care, though, not to create an "alternative party" area.

The Host or Hostess

- This is your chance to take center stage! It is also your chance to look stunning, so you must dress the part.

- It goes without saying that you need to take care of your guests and make sure people have someone to talk to and enough to eat and drink.

- Aim to have all your preparations done well before the party starts so that you don't become—or appear to be—rushed and flustered as people arrive.

- Make sure you plan your entire outfit beforehand so that you are not running around searching for that vital accessory or piece of jewelry at the last minute.

- Resist the urge to drink before your guests arrive so that you can be fresh and entertaining throughout the night. A couple of drinks that slip down before the party can make you too lively for sober arrivals!

- As the party winds down, remember to thank your guests for coming, and tell them to look out for your next event.

Special Occasion Parties

Birthday Party

What better reason to throw a party?! An elegant birthday gathering can be the easiest event you can imagine and the best treat you can give yourself or someone else—the lucky person!

Preparation

- Decide on the guest list—will it be an adult-only old-friends affair, or a grand affair to include family, friends, and work colleagues?

- Send invitations well in advance and choose tasteful designs.

- Reserve a table dressed in suitable linen for gifts, as people are bound to bring them.

- You can prevent chaotic thank-you-note scenarios by opening presents the next morning and keeping a list of whom to thank for what.

A party filled with laughter, storytelling, gift-giving, and fabulous feasting will create long-lasting memories for everyone.

Decor

- Decorate the house with tasteful birthday streamers and, if possible, match them with the table linen and invitations.

- Photographs of you with friends and family through the years, mounted on cork boards, are great fun, especially if you provide some blank boards for others to bring their own photographs.

- Make sure that you arrange a prominent spot to display the birthday cake.

Menu

- The elegant dishes in this chapter are refreshingly simple to create and finger food is an effective way to feed a discerning crowd.

- Serve morsels, such as the Mixed Antipasto Meat Platter (page 27) and Smoked Salmon Pâté Bruschetta (page 19), on oversized platters.

- The pièce de résistance may be a birthday cake (page 31), fabulous dessert, or amazing arrangement of exotic fresh fruits.

Dainty sandwiches in a range of shapes add variety to a buffet table. These are best if they aren't assembled more than 4–6 hours before serving, but the fillings can be made in advance and stored in the refrigerator.

deluxe sandwiches

MAKES 24 of each

for the shrimp salad pinwheels
1½ oz/40 g full-fat soft cheese
4 oz/115 g canned shrimp, drained, rinsed, and finely chopped
1 stalk celery, very finely chopped
1 tbsp mayonnaise
1 tsp tomato purée
1 tsp very finely chopped fresh dill
lemon juice, to taste
salt and white pepper
6 slices white or whole-wheat bread
unsalted butter, softened

for the deviled egg triangles
4 hard-cooked large eggs, shelled and finely chopped
2 tbsp mayonnaise
1 tsp Dijon mustard
pinch cayenne pepper
salt and pepper
unsalted butter, softened
12 slices whole-wheat bread
2 punnets salad cress

for the tuna salad round sandwiches
1 can (7 oz/200 g) tuna in olive oil, drained
3 tbsp mayonnaise
1 large roasted red pepper bottled in oil, rinsed, drained, and finely chopped
finely grated rind of 1 lemon
salt and pepper
unsalted butter, softened
24 thin slices whole-grain bread
small bunch fresh parsley, very finely chopped

Make the sandwiches in advance. To make the shrimp salad, put the cheese in a bowl and beat until smooth. Stir in the shrimp, celery, mayonnaise, tomato purée, and dill. Add lemon juice and salt and white pepper to taste. Cover and chill until required.

To make the deviled egg filling, put the eggs in a bowl, add the mayonnaise, mustard, and cayenne pepper and stir together. Add salt and pepper to taste. Cover and chill until ready to use.

To make the tuna salad, flake the tuna into a bowl and beat in the mayonnaise until well blended. Stir in the red pepper, lemon rind, and salt and pepper to taste.

To make the shrimp salad pinwheels, trim the crusts off the bread and cut each slice into rectangles about 3 x 5½ inches/7.5 x 13 cm. Use a rolling pin to flatten each slice. Use your fingers to press 2 slices together at the short ends, squeezing to seal the edges; repeat to make 3 more long slices. Very lightly spread the slices with butter, then top with the shrimp mixture, taking it to the edges. Working with one long slice at a time, tightly roll up the bread, starting at a short end; repeat with the remaining 3 long slices. Wrap each slice very tightly in plastic wrap and chill for at least 1 hour. When ready to serve, remove from the refrigerator and use a serrated knife to thinly slice off both ends to neaten, then cut 8 slices from each roll.

To make the deviled egg triangles, spread the butter over the bread slices. Spread the deviled egg mixture over 6 of the slices, then snip cress over the tops. Top with the remaining bread slices, buttered sides down. Use a serrated knife to cut off the crusts, then cut each sandwich into 4 triangles. Wrap tightly in plastic wrap and chill until ready to serve. Unwrap and arrange attractively on a plate, then snip more cress over the tops.

To make the tuna salad round sandwiches, spread the butter over the bread slices. Use a 2-inch/5-cm round cutter to cut 2 circles from each slice. (You might be able to get 3 circles from larger slices, in which case you will only need 16 slices.) Spread the tuna mixture over 24 of the circles, then top with the remaining 24 circles, buttered sides down. Use a knife to neaten the edges, then spread very lightly with butter. Roll the buttered edges in the parsley. Stack the sandwiches, then wrap very tightly in plastic wrap and chill until ready to serve. Unwrap and arrange on a plate.

Deliciously rich, these elegant bruschettas are ideal for parties. The poached salmon pâté can be prepared in advance for quick assembly, or serve it separately from the toasts for guests to help themselves.

smoked salmon pâté bruschetta

MAKES 24

1/2 scallion, sliced

1/2 lemon, sliced

1 bay leaf, torn in half

1/2 tsp black peppercorns, lightly crushed

4 fl oz/125 ml dry white wine

1 lb/450 g boneless salmon, cut into pieces

4 oz/115 g butter, at room temperature

5 oz/140 g smoked salmon, cut into bite-size pieces

4 scallions, white parts and half the green parts, very finely chopped

1/4 tsp ground nutmeg

2 tbsp very finely chopped fresh parsley

salt and pepper

24 slices of French bread, each about 1/2 inch/1 cm thick

Put the scallion, lemon slices, bay leaf, peppercorns, and white wine in a large skillet, add water to half fill the skillet, and bring to a boil. Boil for 2 minutes, and then reduce the heat to its lowest setting. Add the salmon pieces, cover the skillet, and leave to simmer for 8 minutes. Remove the skillet from the heat, keep covered, and allow the salmon to cool in the cooking liquid.

Meanwhile, melt 1 oz/30 g of the butter in a large skillet over medium heat. Add the smoked salmon, scallions and nutmeg and stir for about 2 minutes until the salmon looses its shiny coral color and becomes opaque. Remove from the heat and set aside until cool.

Drain and flake the poached salmon and put into a wide, shallow bowl. Add the smoked salmon mixture and cooking juices and the remaining butter and use your fingers to mix it all together until the salmon is very finely mixed. Stir in the parsley. Taste and adjust the seasoning, although you probably won't need much salt because of the flavor of the smoked salmon. Spoon into a bowl, cover, and chill until 30 minutes before you are ready to serve.

When you are ready to serve, preheat the broiler to high. Toast the bread on both sides until golden brown and crisp. Spread the salmon pâté on the hot toast.

Party Tip—If you are hosting a party for someone special, check with the birthday guest who they want to be there—should it be just close friends and family, or work colleagues too?

Make the toppings early in the day and chill them until you are laying out the food. For super-efficient planning, bake the crostini in a fairly cool oven until crisp, then cool and store in an airtight container for up to 5 days prior to the party.

crostini canapés

MAKES 20

1 thin French baguette, sliced

extra-virgin olive oil

for the gorgonzola cheese with caramelized onions

2 large onions, thinly sliced

1 oz/25 g butter

1½ oz/40 g superfine sugar

8 fl oz/225 ml water

6 oz/175 g gorgonzola cheese

for the tomato, avocado & bacon

2 oz/55 g chopped bacon

1 tbsp olive oil

1 large tomato, cored, seeded, and finely diced

1–2 tbsp lemon juice

1–2 tbsp extra-virgin olive oil

2 tbsp finely shredded basil leaves

pinch of sugar

salt and pepper

1 avocado

Preheat the broiler and place the bread slices on the broiler pan about 4 inches/10 cm from the source of the heat. Toast slowly for 6–8 minutes, turning once, until crisp and golden on both sides. Leave to cool.

To make the caramelized onions, put the onions, butter, and half the sugar in a saucepan with the water and bring to a boil. Reduce the heat and simmer, uncovered, for about 20 minutes until the onions are tender and the water has evaporated. Transfer the onions to a frying pan, sprinkle with the remaining sugar, and stir over medium–high heat until the sugar melts and the onions are a light golden brown.

To make the tomato, avocado, and bacon topping, put the chopped bacon and olive oil in a skillet over medium–high heat and stir for about 5 minutes until the bacon is crisp. Remove from the skillet, drain on paper towels, and then transfer to a bowl. Add the diced tomatoes, lemon juice, olive oil, basil, sugar, and salt and pepper to taste and stir. Cut the avocado in half, remove the pit and peel, then finely dice the flesh. Add to the bowl and gently stir together, making sure the avocado is well coated so it doesn't turn brown; add extra lemon juice or olive oil, if necessary.

When ready to serve, cover 10 crostini with a small slice of gorgonzola cheese, then top with a dollop of the caramelized onions. Top the remaining crostini with the tomato, avocado, and bacon mixture. Alternatively, serve the crostini in a large, napkin-lined basket and offer the toppings in separate bowls. Let guests help themselves—be sure to have a couple of teaspoons on saucers beside the bowls of toppings.

There is no reason why you couldn't use fresh crabmeat instead of canned.

crab packages

MAKES 20

12 oz/350 g canned white
crabmeat, drained
1 fresh red chile, seeded and
chopped
4 scallions, sliced finely
1 tbsp red curry paste
juice of 1/2 lime
salt
20 wonton skins
oil for cooking

for the dip
1/4 cup superfine sugar
2 tbsp water
2 tbsp rice wine vinegar
3 pieces preserved ginger,
sliced
1 tbsp ginger syrup from
the jar

Put the crabmeat into a bowl and add the chile, scallions, and curry paste. Stir together with the lime juice and salt to taste.

Put the skins in a pile and put a little crabmeat in the center of the top skin. Brush the edges with a little water and roll up the edges to make a small cigar-shaped package. Continue to make packages with the skins.

Heat the oil in a wok or large skillet and cook the packages, a few at a time, until golden brown. Drain on paper towels.

Put all the ingredients for the dip in a small pan and heat gently until the sugar has dissolved. Serve warm with the crab packages.

Party Tip—When it comes to music, play songs that were hits when the birthday boy or girl first took an interest in dancing and music. Late seventies disco classics and eighties bubblegum pop are great floor-fillers.

The prepared, unfilled chicory leaves can be stored inside a sealed plastic bag in the refrigerator for up to a day.

pretty chicory bites

MAKES 24

3 medium-sized heads chicory

4 oz/125 g bleu cheese, such as Stilton, finely crumbled

4 tbsp pecan halves, very finely chopped

1 punnet salad cress

for the dressing

3½ fl oz/100 ml extra-virgin olive oil

2½ tbsp balsamic vinegar

1 tsp Dijon mustard

1 tsp sugar

salt and pepper

To make the dressing, put the oil, vinegar, mustard, sugar, and salt and pepper to taste in a screw-top jar and shake until blended. Taste and adjust the seasoning, then set aside until ready to use. (The prepared dressing can be stored in the refrigerator for up to 3 days.)

Cut the edges off the chicory heads so you can separate the leaves. Pick over the leaves and select the 24 best, boat-shaped leaves, then rinse them and pat dry.

Put the cheese and pecans in a bowl and gently toss together. Add 2 tablespoons of the dressing and toss again.

Arrange the chicory leaves on serving platters, then put a teaspoon of the cheese and pecans toward the pointed end of each leaf. Add some snipped salad cress to each to garnish. Cover and chill for up to an hour.

The town of San Daniele competes with Parma for the prize for the best cured ham, while Milan stakes its claim for the tastiest salami. Let your party guests' taste buds decide!

mixed antipasto meat platter

SERVES 4

1 cantaloupe

2 oz/55 g Italian salami, sliced thinly

8 slices prosciutto

8 slices bresaola

8 slices mortadella

4 plum tomatoes, sliced thinly

4 fresh figs, halved

2/3 cup pitted black olives

2 tbsp shredded fresh basil leaves

4 tbsp extra-virgin olive oil, plus extra for serving

pepper

Cut the melon in half, scoop out and discard the seeds, then cut the flesh into 8 wedges. Arrange the wedges on one half of a large serving platter.

Arrange the salami, prosciutto, bresaola, and mortadella in loose folds on the other half of the platter. Arrange the tomato slices and fig halves on the platter.

Sprinkle the olives over the antipasto. Sprinkle the basil over the tomatoes and drizzle with olive oil. Season to taste with pepper, then serve with extra olive oil.

Party Tip—Big question: what to serve? Whether it's a small gathering with dainty canapés, or a buffet feast, be sure to include at least one of the favorite foods of the person whose birthday is being celebrated.

These cupcakes, made with a plain base and a buttercream topping, are so light and delicious that you can easily eat more than one!

birthday party cupcakes

MAKES 24

1 cup soft margarine

1¹⁄₈ cups superfine sugar

4 eggs

scant 1³⁄₄ cups self-rising white flour

a selection of candy and chocolates, to garnish

for the buttercream

4 oz/115 g unsalted butter, softened

4 oz/115 g confectioners' sugar, sifted

vanilla extract, to taste

Preheat the oven to 350°F/180°C. Put 24 paper cupcake cases in a muffin pan, or put 24 double thick paper cases on a baking sheet.

Put the margarine, sugar, eggs, and flour in a large bowl and, using a handheld electric mixer, beat together until just smooth. Spoon the batter into the paper cases.

Bake the cupcakes in the preheated oven for 15–20 minutes, or until well risen, golden brown, and firm to the touch. Transfer to a wire rack and let cool.

To make the frosting, put the butter in a bowl and beat until fluffy. Sift in the confectioners' sugar and the vanilla extract to taste, and beat together until smooth and creamy.

When the cupcakes are cool, spread the frosting on top of each cupcake, then decorate with the candy and chocolates of your choice.

Party Tip—To frost the birthday cake perfectly, spread a thin layer over the cake, and then refrigerate until it's firm. Remove from the refrigerator and continue frosting. Viola! Crumb-free professional icing!

No birthday celebration is complete without a birthday cake and sparkling candles. Anyone can bake this simple, fun cake.

dotty celebration cake

SERVES 6–8

8 oz/225 g butter, softened

8 oz/225 g superfine sugar

4 eggs

8 oz/225 g self-rising flour

1 tsp vanilla extract

2 oz/60 g strawberry or raspberry preserves

for the buttercream filling and topping

7 oz/200 g butter, softened

14 oz/400 g confectioners' sugar

1 tbsp milk

vanilla extract, to taste

3 1/2 oz/100 g sugar paste or prepared icing, colored and rolled, and cut into circles using a round cutter

Preheat oven to 350°F/180°C. Grease and line two 8-inch/20-cm round cake pans with baking parchment.

Place the butter and sugar in a bowl and beat well, either by hand or with an electric mixer, until pale and soft. Gradually beat in the eggs, adding a spoonful of the flour to prevent the mixture from curdling. Use a metal spoon to fold in the remaining flour and the vanilla extract.

Divide the mixture evenly between the two pans and spread out.

Bake in the oven for about 25 minutes, until well risen and springy to the touch.

Leave the sponge cakes to cool in the pans for a few minutes, and then turn out onto wire racks and leave to cool. Peel off the paper.

Make the buttercream by creaming the butter with the confectioners' sugar until pale and soft. Finally beat in the milk and vanilla extract to taste.

When the cakes are cool, sandwich them together with the preserves and a third of the buttercream. Place on a 10-inch/25-cm cake board or plate.

Spread the remaining buttercream over the top and sides of the cake, using a palette knife to give a smooth finish.

Arrange different colored circles of sugar paste or prepared icing all over the top and sides of the cake. Add candles to finish.

For a fragrant twist, substitute dry ginger ale for sparkling water or, for an alcoholic version, replace the sparkling water with sparkling white wine.

citrus punch

SERVES 2

4 tbsp orange juice
1 tbsp lime juice
scant 1/2 cup sparkling water
4 ice cubes
12 oz/350 g frozen summer berries, such as blueberries, raspberries, and strawberries
whole fresh strawberries, raspberries, and blueberries on toothpicks, to garnish

Pour the orange juice, lime juice, and sparkling water into a blender or food processor and process gently until combined.

Put the ice cubes between 2 clean cloths and crush with a rolling pin. Add to the blender with the frozen berries and process until a slushy consistency has been reached.

Pour the mixture into glasses, then garnish with whole strawberries, raspberries, and blueberries on toothpicks and serve.

Party Tip—Make your party truly memorable by leaving a "birthday book" around for guests to write in if they wish—it's sure to be a source of amusement as the night draws to a close.

Sangria has a refreshing fruit flavor that belies its potency, although you can always reduce the alcoholic content by adding more club soda or lemonade.

sangria

SERVES 6

1 bottle full-bodied red wine

3 tbsp Cointreau

3 tbsp brandy

juice of 1 orange and 1 lime

1 tbsp superfine sugar, or to taste

1 orange

1 lime

1 peach or red-skinned apple

10 fl oz/300 ml soda water or lemonade

30–36 cracked ice cubes

Pour the wine into a large pitcher or punch bowl. Add the Cointreau, brandy, and orange and lime juices, then stir in the sugar. Cover and leave to chill in the refrigerator for 2 hours. (This can be prepared several hours in advance if convenient.)

Cut the orange and lime into thin slices and store in a covered bowl in the refrigerator for several hours if necessary. When ready to serve, cut the peach in half, remove and discard the pit and slice the flesh. Alternatively, cut the apple in half, remove and discard the core, and thinly slice. Remove the sangria from the refrigerator and stir in the sliced fruit.

To serve, add the soda water or lemonade and ice cubes, stir well, then pour or ladle into glasses.

Party Tip— Party punch or pitchers of blended drinks make a refreshing and economical choice. Buy flavored waters and sparkling fruit juices for your guests who are not drinking alcohol.

New Year's Eve Party

*H*erald the New Year in style with lots of glitz and glamor. It's the biggest night of the year, so make yours the biggest party—start the new year as you mean to continue it!

Preparation

- Try to plan everything well in advance—before Christmas, or even Thanksgiving, as December can be one of the most chaotic months of the year, and many people will have several options when it comes to that countdown.

- Plan practical food choices and buy all your ingredients in advance to avoid a last-minute rush around the supermarket.

- On party night, set an alarm to give a ten-minute warning before midnight to avoid missing that special moment.

The end of one year and the start of a new one is cause for revelry. Host a fabulous New Year's Eve party that your guests will never forget!

Decor

- Streamline the Christmas decor with elegant colors, such as silver and black; try to avoid green and red tinsel for this particular night.
- Avoid harsh lighting to encourage the party atmosphere to continue well into the small hours of New Year.
- Lay out party poppers and streamers to guarantee that guests mark midnight with a bang.

Menu

- These exciting but undemanding recipes will guarantee that everyone is in festive spirits and you're not stuck in the kitchen until next year!
- Spread stylish servings of Spinach, Feta & Tomato Triangles (page 46) and Soft-Wrapped Pork & Shrimp Rolls (page 41) strategically around the main party area and kitchen to avoid a traffic jam around a main buffet table.
- The Bubbly Peach & Mint Tea Punch (page 57) will go down wonderfully as the festivities really get going, so make sure you have plenty of supplies!

hummus, tapenade, guacamole & aïoli dips

SERVES 4–6

hummus

8 oz/225 g dried chickpeas, drained

2/3 cup tahini paste

4–6 tbsp virgin olive oil

4–6 tbsp lemon juice

2–3 garlic cloves, crushed

1–2 tbsp hot water

salt and pepper

carrot sticks, celery sticks, and cucumber sticks, to serve

To make the hummus, put all the ingredients, except the water and salt and pepper, into a food processor and process to form a smooth paste. Using the pulse button, slowly blend in the hot water to give a dipping consistency. Add salt and pepper to taste.

SERVES 4–6

aïoli

3 large garlic cloves, finely chopped

2 egg yolks

1 cup extra-virgin olive oil

1 tbsp lemon juice

1 tbsp lime juice

1 tbsp Dijon mustard

1 tbsp chopped fresh tarragon

salt and pepper

1 fresh tarragon sprig, to garnish

To make the aïoli, make sure that all the ingredients are at room temperature. Place the garlic and egg yolks in a food processor and process until smooth. With the motor running, pour in the oil, a little at a time, until the mixture begins to thicken, then pour in the remaining oil in a thin stream until a thick mayonnaise forms. Add the lemon and lime juices, mustard, and tarragon and season with salt and pepper to taste. Pulse to mix and then serve.

SERVES 4–6

guacamole

2 large, ripe avocados

juice of 1 lime, or to taste

2 tsp olive oil

1/2 onion, finely chopped

1 fresh green chile, such as poblano, seeded and finely chopped

1 garlic clove, crushed

1/4 tsp ground cumin

1 tbsp chopped fresh cilantro, plus extra to garnish

salt and pepper

To make the guacamole, cut the avocados in half lengthwise, and remove their pits. Peel, then roughly chop and place in a non-metallic bowl. Squeeze over the lime juice and add the oil. Mash the avocados with a fork to the desired consistency—either chunky or smooth. Stir in the onion, chile, garlic, cumin, and chopped cilantro, then season to taste with salt and pepper. Serve sprinkled with extra chopped cilantro.

SERVES 4–6

tapenade

3 1/2 oz/100 g canned anchovy fillets

12 oz/350 g black olives, pitted and coarsely chopped

2 garlic cloves, coarsely chopped

2 tbsp capers, drained and rinsed

1 tbsp Dijon mustard

3 tbsp extra-virgin olive oil

2 tbsp lemon juice

Drain the anchovies, reserving the oil from the can. Coarsely chop the fish and place in the blender. Add the reserved oil and all the remaining ingredients. Process to a smooth puree. Stop and scrape down the sides if necessary. Transfer the tapenade to a dish, cover with plastic wrap, and chill in the refrigerator until ready to serve.

Party Tip—Serve dips in nonmetalic bowls with a selection of raw vegetables and breadsticks.

These rolls can be prepared ahead of a party, or alternatively you can lay out the ingredients so that guests can roll their own wraps and fillings.

soft-wrapped pork & shrimp rolls

MAKES 20

4 oz/115 g firm tofu

3 tbsp vegetable or peanut oil

1 tsp finely chopped garlic

2 oz/55 g lean pork, shredded

4 oz/115 g raw shrimp, peeled and deveined

1/2 small carrot, cut into short thin sticks

1/2 cup fresh or canned bamboo shoots, rinsed and shredded (if using fresh shoots, boil in water first for 30 minutes)

1 cup very finely sliced cabbage

1/2 cup snow peas, julienned

1-egg omelet, shredded

1 tsp salt

1 tsp light soy sauce

1 tsp Chinese rice wine

pinch of white pepper

20 soft spring roll skins

chili bean sauce, to serve

Slice the tofu horizontally into thin slices and cook in 1 tablespoon of the oil until it turns golden brown. Cut into thin strips and set aside.

In a preheated wok or large frying pan, heat the remaining oil and stir-fry the garlic until fragrant. Add the pork and stir for about 1 minute, then add the shrimp and stir for an additional minute. One by one, stirring well after each, add the carrot, bamboo shoots, cabbage, snow peas, tofu, and, finally, the shredded omelet. Season with the salt, light soy sauce, rice wine, and pepper. Stir for an additional minute, then turn into a serving dish.

To assemble each roll, smear a skin with a little chili bean sauce and place a heaping teaspoon of the filling toward the bottom of the circle. Roll up the bottom edge to secure the filling, turn in the sides, and continue to roll up gently, from the bottom.

Once cooled, the frittata can be cut into wedges or small squares. Provide toothpicks so that guests can spear the frittata squares for quick and easy snacking on the move.

chorizo & olive frittata

SERVES 4

1/4 cup butter

1 small onion, chopped finely

1 small green or red bell pepper, seeded and chopped finely

2 tomatoes, seeded and diced

2 small cooked potatoes, diced

4 1/2 oz/125 g chorizo or salami, chopped finely

8 green or black olives, pitted and chopped finely

8 large eggs

2 tbsp milk

salt and pepper

1/2 cup Cheddar cheese, grated

mixed salad greens and pimiento strips, to garnish

Melt the butter over medium heat in a large skillet. Add the onion, bell pepper, and tomatoes. Stir well to coat in butter, then cook for 3–4 minutes, or until soft. Mix in the potatoes, chorizo, and olives. Cook gently for 5 minutes to heat through.

In a small bowl, beat the eggs with the milk and salt and pepper to taste. Pour over the vegetables in the skillet and reduce the heat to low. Cook the eggs, occasionally lifting the edges and tilting the skillet to let the liquid run to the outside.

Preheat the broiler to high. When the eggs are mostly set, with only a small wet patch in the middle, sprinkle over the cheese. Place the skillet under the broiler and cook for 2 minutes, or until the cheese has melted and is golden brown. Remove the skillet from the broiler and let the fritatta cool before cutting into wedges or squares. Garnish with salad greens and pimiento strips, then serve.

Sushi rice is medium-grain rice that is slightly sticky when cooked. The long-grain varieties that become dry and fluffy are no good for sushi because they do not stick together.

pressed sushi bars with smoked salmon & cucumber

MAKES 8–10

for the rice
½ quantity freshly cooked sushi rice
6 fl oz/175 ml cup water
½ sheet kombu (optional)
1 tbsp sushi rice seasoning

for the topping
2 tbsp Japanese mayonnaise
7 oz/200 g smoked salmon
½ cucumber, peeled and cut into very thin slices

Wash the sushi rice under cold running water until the water runs clear and then drain the rice. Put the rice in a pan with the water and the kombu, if using, cover and bring to a boil as quickly as you can. Remove the kombu, then turn the heat down and simmer for 10 minutes with the lid on. Do not at any point take the lid off the pan once you have removed the kombu. Turn off the heat and let the rice stand for 15 minutes.

Put the hot rice in a large, very shallow bowl and pour the sushi rice seasoning evenly over the surface of the rice. You will need to use both hands, one to mix the seasoning into the rice with quick cutting strokes using a spatula and the other to fan the sushi rice in order to cool it down as quickly as you can. Mix the seasoning in carefully—you do not want to break a single rice grain.

The sushi rice should look shiny and be at room temperature when you are ready to use it.

Meanwhile, oil a terrine pan (preferably with drop-down sides) and line it with a piece of plastic wrap so that the plastic wrap hangs over the edges. This is to help you pull the sushi out afterward. Pack the rice into the pan in a 1¼-inch/3-cm layer then spread a layer of the mayonnaise on top.

Arrange the smoked salmon and cucumber in diagonal strips on top of the rice, doubling up the smoked salmon layers if you have enough so that the topping is nice and thick. Cover the top of the rice with a strip of plastic wrap, put another terrine pan on top and add something heavy, such as a couple of cans of tomatoes, to weigh it down.

Chill the sushi for 15 minutes, then take off the pan and weights and pull out the sushi. Cut the sushi into 8–10 pieces with a wet, sharp knife.

These delicious treats are perfect for parties. Serve them piled high on large platters so guests can help themselves.

spinach, feta & tomato triangles

MAKES 12

2 tbsp olive oil

2 tbsp finely chopped shallot

1 1/3 cups fresh spinach, washed and shredded

salt and pepper

2 sheets filo pastry

1/2 cup feta cheese, crumbled

6 sun-dried tomatoes, chopped finely

1/2 cup butter, melted

Preheat the oven to 400°F/200°C. Heat the oil in a skillet over medium heat and cook the shallot for 2–3 minutes. Add the spinach, then increase the heat to high and cook, stirring constantly, for 2–3 minutes. Remove from the heat and drain in a sieve. Chop coarsely, then season to taste with salt and pepper and let cool.

Cut each sheet of pastry into 6 strips. Place a spoonful of spinach at the bottom of each strip. Scatter cheese and tomatoes on top. Fold the bottom right-hand corner of each strip up to meet the opposite side to form a triangle. Fold the triangle toward the top of the strip and repeat until you reach the top of the strip.

Brush the edges of each triangle with melted butter, then transfer to a greased cookie sheet. Brush the top of the parcel with more butter. Place the cookie sheet in the oven and bake for 10 minutes, or until the pastry is golden and crisp. Remove from the oven and serve immediately. Alternatively, cool the triangles on a wire rack and serve warm or cold.

Party Tip—Fill deflated balloons that match your party decor with large amounts of confetti by inserting a funnel into the mouth of each balloon. Fill the balloons with helium and tie with a colored ribbon. Let the balloons float up to the ceiling. At midnight, encourage everyone to pull down the balloons and pop them.

These toasts are very easy to prepare, yet make very impressive party food.

basil zucchini toast

SERVES 4

4 slices of white bread
1/4 cup butter, melted
4 eggs
2 cups milk
1 small onion, chopped finely
1 zucchini, grated
1 cup grated Cheddar cheese
1 cup fresh breadcrumbs
1 tbsp finely chopped fresh basil
salt and pepper
pinch of paprika
2 tbsp grated Parmesan cheese
4 basil leaves, to garnish

Preheat the oven to 375°F/190°C.

Remove the crusts from the bread and press the slices into the cups of a muffin pan. Brush well with melted butter.

Beat the eggs well in a medium mixing bowl. Stir in the milk. Add the onion, zucchini, cheese, breadcrumbs, basil, and salt and pepper to taste. Mix well.

Carefully spoon the egg mixture into the bread cases. Sprinkle with the paprika and Parmesan cheese, then place the pan in the oven and bake for about 45 minutes, or until set and golden.

Turn off the oven, but leave the toasts to cool for 10 minutes before transferring them to a serving platter. Garnish each with a basil leaf before serving.

These are an excellent choice for vegetarian guests or anyone who loves spicy food. They can be served warm, or at room temperature.

omelet rolls

SERVES 4

4 large eggs
2 tbsp water
1 tbsp Thai soy sauce
6 scallions, chopped finely
1 fresh red chile, seeded and
chopped finely
1 tbsp vegetable or
peanut oil
1 tbsp green curry paste
bunch of fresh cilantro,
chopped, plus leaves
to garnish

Beat the eggs with the water and Thai soy sauce in a bowl. Set aside. Mix together the scallions and chopped chile.

Heat half the oil in an 8-inch skillet and pour in half the egg mixture. Tilt to coat the bottom of the skillet evenly and cook until set. Lift out and set aside. Heat the remaining oil and make a second omelet in the same way.

Spread the scallion and chile mixture and curry paste in a thin layer over each omelet and sprinkle the cilantro on top. Roll up tightly. Cut each roll in half and then cut each piece on the diagonal in half again. Serve immediately, while still warm, or prepare in advance and serve at room temperature. Garnish with cilantro leaves.

Party Tip— Take guests' coats as soon as they enter and hang them on a coat rack, in a closet, or lay them across a bed in an unused bedroom. Show guests where you put them so they can help themselves when leaving, causing less disruption to you and other guests.

Cover the individual bowls with plastic wrap and chill the mousse in the refrigerator for at least 3 hours before serving. This is a good recipe to make the day before a party.

chocolate mousse

SERVES 4–6

8 squares bittersweet chocolate, chopped

2 tbsp brandy, Grand Marnier, or Cointreau

4 tbsp water

1 oz/25 g unsalted butter, diced

3 large eggs, separated

1/4 tsp cream of tartar

1/4 cup sugar

1/2 cup heavy cream

Place the chocolate, brandy, and water in a small pan over low heat and melt, stirring, until smooth. Remove the pan from the heat and beat in the butter.

Beat the egg yolks into the chocolate mixture, one after another, until blended, then let cool slightly.

Meanwhile, using an electric mixer on low speed, beat the egg whites in a spotlessly clean bowl until they are frothy, then gradually increase the mixer's speed and beat until soft peaks form. Sprinkle the cream of tartar over the surface, then add the sugar, tablespoon by tablespoon, and continue beating until stiff peaks form. Beat several tablespoons of the egg whites into the chocolate mixture to loosen.

In another bowl, whip the cream until soft peaks form. Spoon the cream over the chocolate mixture, then spoon the remaining whites over the cream. Use a large metal spoon or rubber spatula to fold the chocolate into the cream and egg whites.

Either spoon the chocolate mousse into a large serving bowl or divide among 4 or 6 individual bowls. Cover with plastic wrap and chill the mousse for at least 3 hours before serving.

Once made, the pavlova can be stored in an airtight container and kept in the refrigerator for up to 2 days.

chocolate & raspberry pavlova

SERVES 6

4 egg whites
1 cup superfine sugar
1 tsp cornstarch
1 tsp white wine vinegar
1 tsp vanilla extract
1¼ cups heavy cream,
1 tbsp superfine sugar,
2 tbsp framboise liqueur,
1 cup fresh raspberries,
and 2 oz/55 g bittersweet
chocolate, shaved, to serve

Preheat the oven to 300°F/150°C. In a large mixing bowl, using an electric mixer, beat the egg whites until stiff and gradually beat in a generous ½ cup of the sugar. In a separate bowl, mix the remaining sugar with the cornstarch and then beat it into the egg white mixture; it should be very shiny and firm. Quickly fold the vinegar and vanilla extract into the egg white mixture.

Draw a 10-inch/25-cm circle on a sheet of baking paper, turn the paper over, and place it on a baking tray. Pile the meringue onto the baking paper and spread evenly to the edge of the circle; swirl it around on top to make an attractive shape. Bake in the center of the preheated oven for 1 hour.

Remove from the oven, cool slightly, then peel off the parchment. Place the pavlova on a large serving plate. It will shrink and crack, but do not worry about this.

One hour before serving, whip together the cream, sugar, and liqueur until thick and floppy. Pile on top of the pavlova and decorate with raspberries and shaved chocolate. Chill before serving.

Party Tip—New Year's Eve just wouldn't be New Year's Eve without them, so supply plenty of horns, party poppers, and confetti.

For a pretty touch, half-fill each indentation in an ice-cube tray with water and freeze until almost frozen. Remove from the freezer and add a flower petal to each ice cube before returning the tray to the freezer until solid.

bubbly peach & mint tea punch

SERVES 24

16 fl oz/450 ml water
2 tea bags
1 oz/25 g fresh mint leaves
3 1/2 oz/100 g superfine sugar
6 fl oz/175 ml good-quality lemonade, chilled
12 fl oz/350 ml peach nectar, chilled
35 fl oz/1 liter bottle ginger ale, chilled
35 fl oz/1 liter bottle soda water, chilled
ice cubes, to serve

Bring the water to a boil in a saucepan over a high heat. Remove from the heat, add the tea bags and mint leaves, and leave to steep for 15 minutes. Remove and discard the tea bags, then leave the mint leaves in the liquid until it is cool.

Meanwhile, put the sugar in another pan, add 4 tablespoons water, and stir until the sugar dissolves, then bring to a boil, without stirring, and boil for 4 minutes. Remove from the heat and leave to cool completely.

Strain the mint-flavored liquid into a bowl or pitcher. Stir in the cooled syrup, cover, and chill until ready to serve.

When you're ready to serve, mix all the chilled ingredients together in a large punch bowl. Add the ice cubes and serve.

As midnight draws closer, there is nothing like the fizz of a champagne cocktail. Break out the champagne and spoil your guests with these little sparklers.

kir royale

SERVES 1

few drops of crème de cassis, or to taste
1 tbsp brandy (optional)
champagne, chilled

Pour the crème de cassis and brandy, if using, into a chilled flute.

Wait a moment, and then gently pour in the champagne.

Party Tip—As the hostess, it's only right that you make a toast. Choose a point at the beginning of the evening to welcome everyone, or just before the chimes, tap your glass to get attention, thank your guests for coming, and be the first to wish them a fabulous New Year.

Mardi Gras Party

With all the parades, decorations, and festivities, the merriment of a Mardi Gras Party is not to be missed. What better inspiration do you need? It's colorful, lively, and excessive—just like any good party should be!

Preparation

- Decide in advance whether your party is going to get into the full swing of the Mardi Gras spirit and be fancy dress. If so, give guests plenty of notice to sort those costumes out!

- Provide masks and tasteful garlands to get everyone involved in the revelry.

Decor

- Color is the order of the day—this is definitely not a minimalist occasion!

- Add fun and flamboyant touches with streamers, confetti, and flags.

Experience the feeling of Mardi Gras with your very own party. Be colorful and outlandish—anything goes so long as you live the night to the fullest!

- Be daring with your table linen—try a bold tablecloth with multicolored placemats.
- Try making some decorations from cut fresh fruits interspersed with edible flower heads.

Music

- Think "carnival-on-the-Copacabana" or "New Orleans" with salsa, samba, and Dixieland jazz setting the scene.
- Loud and lively music is great as the party gets going but keep the volume to a reasonable level during the meal, allowing people to chat and compliment the host or hostess on the wonderful spread!

Menu

- The spicy and sensuous cuisine in this chapter will give the party some real fiesta flavor.
- Serve up delectable Chicken Gumbo (page 62) and Jambalaya (page 65) in giant dishes to allow everyone to help themselves and have a ball!
- End the evening on a note of ultimate indulgence with the irresistible Mississippi Mud Pie (page 77).

A cross between a soup and a stew, gumbo is a great dish for a Mardi Gras celebration.

chicken gumbo

SERVES 4–6

1 chicken, weighing 3 lb 5 oz/
1.5 kg, cut into 6 pieces

2 celery stalks, 1 broken in
half and 1 finely chopped

1 carrot, chopped

2 onions, 1 sliced and
1 chopped

2 bay leaves

salt

4 tbsp corn or peanut oil

1/3 cup all-purpose flour

2 large garlic cloves,
crushed

1 green bell pepper, seeded
and diced

1 lb/450 g fresh okra,
trimmed, then cut crosswise
into 1/2-inch/1-cm slices

8 oz/225 g andouille
sausage or Polish kielbasa,
sliced

2 tbsp tomato paste

1 tsp dried thyme

1/2 tsp salt

1/2 tsp cayenne pepper

1/4 tsp pepper

14 oz/400 g canned peeled
plum tomatoes

cooked long-grain rice,
to serve

Put the chicken into a large pan with water to cover, place over medium–high heat, and bring to a boil, skimming the surface to remove the foam. When the foam stops rising, reduce the heat to medium, add the celery stalk halves, carrot, sliced onion, 1 bay leaf, and 1/4 teaspoon of salt and simmer for 30 minutes, or until the chicken is tender and the juices run clear when a skewer is inserted into the thickest part of the meat. Remove the chicken, straining and reserving 1 3/4 pints/1 liter of the liquid. When the chicken is cool enough to handle, remove and discard the skin, bones, and other ingredients. Cut the chicken flesh into bite-sized pieces and reserve.

Heat the oil in a large pan over medium–high heat for 2 minutes. Reduce the heat to low, sprinkle in the flour, and stir to make a roux. Stir constantly until the roux turns hazelnut-brown. If black specks appear, it is burned and you will have to start again.

Add the chopped celery, chopped onion, garlic, bell pepper, and okra to the pan. Increase the heat to medium–high and cook, stirring frequently, for 5 minutes. Add the sausage and cook, stirring frequently, for 2 minutes.

Stir in all the remaining ingredients, including the second bay leaf, and the reserved cooking liquid. Bring to a boil, crushing the tomatoes with a wooden spoon. Reduce the heat to medium–low and let simmer, uncovered, for 30 minutes, stirring occasionally.

Add the chicken to the pan and let simmer for an additional 30 minutes. Taste and adjust the seasoning, if necessary. Discard the bay leaf, spoon the gumbo over the rice, and serve.

The title sounds fun, the food is spicy, and the dish is a festive treat.

jambalaya

SERVES 6

2 tbsp lard or butter

3 lb 5 oz/1.5 kg chicken pieces

2½ tbsp all-purpose flour

8 oz/225 g rindless smoked ham, diced

1 onion, chopped

1 orange bell pepper, seeded and sliced

12 oz/350 g tomatoes, peeled and chopped

1 garlic clove, finely chopped

1 tsp chopped fresh thyme

12 raw peeled jumbo shrimp

1 cup long-grain rice

16 fl oz/450 ml chicken stock or water

dash of Tabasco sauce

salt and pepper

3 scallions, finely chopped

2 tbsp chopped fresh flat-leaf parsley, plus extra sprigs, to garnish

Melt the lard in a large, flameproof casserole. Add the chicken and cook over medium heat, turning occasionally, for 8–10 minutes until golden brown all over. Transfer the chicken to a plate using tongs.

Add the flour to the casserole and cook over very low heat, stirring, until golden brown. Do not let it burn. Return the chicken pieces to the casserole with the ham, onion, bell pepper, tomatoes, garlic, and thyme. Cook, stirring frequently, for 10 minutes.

Stir in the shrimp, rice, and stock, and season to taste with Tabasco and salt and pepper. Bring the mixture to a boil, reduce the heat, cover, and cook for 15–20 minutes until all of the liquid has been absorbed and the rice is tender. Stir in the scallions and chopped parsley, garnish with parsley sprigs, and serve.

Party Tip—Scents are essential, so focus on fresh citrus aromas, jasmine, and ylang ylang essential oils for use in oil burners and potpourri. There is even a Mardi Gras fragrance available!

Do not fry too many squid rings at one time. This causes the oil temperature to drop and they will become soggy. Also avoid over-cooking as the squid will become tough and rubbery rather than moist and tender.

calamari

SERVES 4–6

1 lb/450 g prepared squid
all-purpose flour, for coating
sunflower oil, for
deep-frying
salt
lemon wedges, to garnish

Slice the squid into ¹/₂-inch/1-cm rings and halve the tentacles if large. Rinse under cold running water and dry well with paper towels. Dust the squid rings with flour so that they are lightly coated.

Heat the oil in a deep-fat fryer, large, heavy-bottom pan, or wok to 350–375°F/180–190°C, or until a cube of bread browns in 30 seconds. Deep-fry the squid rings in small batches for 2–3 minutes, or until golden brown and crisp all over, turning several times.

Remove with a slotted spoon and drain well on paper towels. Keep warm in a low oven while you deep-fry the remaining squid rings.

Sprinkle the fried squid rings with salt and serve piping hot, garnished with lemon wedges for squeezing over.

Serve fried catfish fillets for an authentic Mardi Gras feast. For a truly southern feel, coleslaw is a popular accompaniment.

fried catfish

SERVES 4

1/2 cup all-purpose flour
2 eggs
1 1/2 cups yellow cornmeal
1/2 tsp dried thyme
pinch of cayenne pepper
salt and pepper
2 lb/900 g catfish fillets, skinned, rinsed, and patted dry
corn oil, for pan-frying
coleslaw, to serve

Put the flour onto a plate. Beat the eggs in a wide, shallow bowl. Put the cornmeal onto a separate plate and season with the thyme, cayenne pepper, and salt and pepper to taste.

Dust the catfish fillets with the flour on both sides, shaking off any excess, and dip into the eggs, then pat the cornmeal onto both sides.

Heat about 2 inches/5 cm of oil in a large skillet over medium heat. Add as many catfish fillets as will fit without overcrowding the skillet and cook for 2 minutes, or until the coating is golden brown.

Turn the catfish fillets over and cook for an additional 2 minutes, or until golden on both sides. Remove from the skillet with a slotted spoon and drain on paper towels. Transfer the fillets to a low oven to keep warm while you cook the remaining fillets, if necessary. Add more oil to the skillet as needed.

For a true southern meal, serve the fried catfish with coleslaw.

Party Tip— Remember food safety. Always keep cold food cold and hot food hot. Summer heat can quickly turn good food into a health hazard if not served under the correct conditions, so remove perishable dishes from the refrigerator just before serving them.

This dish of poached shrimp with piquant rusty-red sauce is a New Orleans classic and a must for a Mardi Gras celebration.

shrimp remoulade

SERVES 4–6

1½ tbsp salt

1 lemon, sliced

1 lb 12 oz/800 g raw unpeeled large shrimp

shredded iceberg lettuce, 2 shelled hard-cooked eggs, sliced and 2 tomatoes, sliced, to serve

for the remoulade sauce

2 oz/55 g scallions, coarsely chopped

2 oz/55 g celery stalks, coarsely chopped

1 large garlic clove

4 tbsp chopped fresh parsley

2 tbsp Creole mustard or German mustard

2 tbsp superfine sugar

2 tbsp cider vinegar or ketchup

1½ tbsp prepared horseradish

1 tbsp paprika

½ tsp cayenne pepper

½ tsp salt

¼ tsp ground black pepper

few drops of hot pepper sauce, to taste

about ⅔ cup corn or peanut oil

To make the sauce, put the scallions, celery, garlic, and parsley into a food processor and pulse until finely chopped. Add the mustard, sugar, vinegar, horseradish, paprika, cayenne pepper, salt, pepper, and hot pepper sauce to taste and whiz until well blended. With the motor running, pour in the oil through the feed tube in a slow, steady stream until a thick, creamy sauce forms. Transfer to a large bowl, cover, and set aside.

To poach the shrimp, put the salt and lemon slices in a large skillet of water and bring to a boil over high heat. Reduce the heat so that the water simmers gently. Add the shrimp and cook for 3–5 minutes, or until they turn pink.

Drain the shrimp well and rinse them under cold water until cooled. Peel and devein them, adding them to the sauce as you go. Stir together, then cover and let chill for at least 45 minutes, but ideally overnight. Serve on a bed of lettuce with hard-cooked eggs and sliced tomatoes.

Only a small amount of mayonnaise is used to bind the ingredients, so allow plenty of chilling time, which makes handling easier.

crab cakes

SERVES 4

3 eggs

2 scallions, finely chopped

3 tbsp mayonnaise

1 tbsp Dijon mustard

1 tbsp bottled grated horseradish

1 tbsp bottled capers, rinsed, drained, and chopped

1 tbsp chopped fresh parsley

1/2 tsp salt

1/4 tsp pepper

pinch of cayenne pepper, or to taste

1 lb/450 g cooked fresh crabmeat, picked over, or thawed and patted dry if frozen

1/2 cup milk

1/2 cup all-purpose flour

2 cups fine dried white breadcrumbs

up to 4 tbsp butter, for pan-frying

corn oil, for pan-frying

lime wedges, to serve

Combine one of the eggs, the scallions, mayonnaise, mustard, horseradish, capers, parsley, salt, pepper, and cayenne pepper in a bowl and beat together. Stir in the crabmeat, then cover and chill for at least 30 minutes.

Meanwhile, beat the remaining eggs with the milk in a wide, shallow bowl. Put the flour and breadcrumbs onto separate plates. With wet hands, shape the crabmeat mixture into 8 equal balls and form into patties about 1 inch/2.5 cm thick. If the crab cakes feel too soft to hold their shape, return them to the refrigerator for 15 minutes; otherwise proceed with the next step.

Lightly dust a crab cake with flour on both sides. Dip into the egg mixture, then pat the breadcrumbs onto both sides. Continue until all the crab cakes are coated. Cover them and let chill for at least 45 minutes.

Melt 2 tablespoons of the butter with 1/2 inch/1 cm of oil in a large skillet over medium heat. Add as many crab cakes as will fit without overcrowding the skillet and cook for 3 minutes on each side, or until golden brown and crisp.

Remove the crab cakes from the skillet with a slotted spoon and drain on paper towels. Transfer to a low oven to keep warm while you cook the remaining crab cakes. Add more butter and oil to the skillet as needed. When all the crab cakes are cooked, serve with lime wedges.

Party Tip — Use a patio heater for outdoor parties in spring and fall. It's an essential tool for keeping your guests comfortable in the yard when the evenings turn cooler. It will also make sure that the party keeps on going, even after sundown.

Also known as ladies' fingers because of their shape, okra are long green, angular pods with a slightly fuzzy skin. They contain small, pale edible seeds.

deep-fried okra

SERVES 4

1 lb/450 g fresh okra, trimmed and cut into ½-inch/1-cm thick slices

about 4 tbsp water

½ cup yellow cornmeal

3 tbsp self-rising or all-purpose flour

salt and pepper

vegetable oil, for deep-frying

Put the okra into a bowl, sprinkle over the water, and gently stir the okra to just moisten.

Put the cornmeal, flour, salt, and pepper to taste into a plastic bag, hold closed, and shake to mix. Add the okra slices to the bag and shake until lightly coated.

Heat at least 2 inches/5 cm of oil in a deep skillet or pan over high heat until the temperature reaches 350–375°F/180–190°C, or until a cube of bread browns in 30 seconds. Add as many okra slices as will fit without overcrowding the skillet and cook, stirring occasionally, for 2 minutes, or until the okra is bright green and the cornmeal coating is golden yellow.

Remove the okra from the oil with a slotted spoon and drain on paper towels. Reheat the oil, if necessary, and cook the remaining okra.

Serve the okra slices hot as a side dish, or serve hot or cold as a snack.

Sinfully delicious, this gooey, decadent delight has a rich chocolate filling and a crumbly chocolate crust —perfect for a special occasion.

mississippi mud pie

SERVES 4

for the pie dough
scant 1⅝ cups all-purpose flour, plus extra for dusting
2 tbsp unsweetened cocoa
5 oz/140 g butter
2 tbsp superfine sugar
1–2 tbsp cold water

for the filling
6 oz/175 g butter
scant 1¾ cups packed brown sugar
4 eggs, lightly beaten
4 tbsp unsweetened cocoa, sifted
5½ oz/150 g semisweet chocolate
1¼ cups light cream
1 tsp chocolate extract

to garnish
scant 2 cups heavy cream, whipped
chocolate flakes and curls

To make the pie dough, sift the flour and cocoa into a mixing bowl. Rub in the butter with your fingertips until the mixture resembles fine breadcrumbs. Stir in the sugar and enough cold water to mix to a soft dough. Wrap the dough and let chill in the refrigerator for 15 minutes.

Preheat the oven to 375°F/190°C. Roll out the dough on a lightly floured counter and use to line a 9-inch/23-cm loose-bottom tart pan or ceramic pie dish. Line with parchment paper and fill with dried beans. Bake in the oven for 15 minutes. Remove from the oven and take out the paper and beans. Bake the pastry shell for an additional 10 minutes, then remove from the oven and cool on a wire rack.

To make the filling, beat the butter and sugar together in a bowl and gradually beat in the eggs with the cocoa. Melt the chocolate and beat it into the mixture with the light cream and the chocolate extract.

Reduce the oven temperature to 325°F/160°C. Pour the mixture into the pastry shell and bake for 45 minutes, or until the filling has set.

Let the mud pie cool completely, then transfer it to a serving plate, if you like. Cover with the whipped cream. Garnish the pie with chocolate flakes and curls and then let chill until ready to serve.

Party Tip— Mardi Gras beads are the "must-have" item of the night, but they definitely don't have to be the tacky kind. Search local boutiques or Internet stores and then adorn each guest with beads on their arrival.

This famous cocktail was invented around 1905 in a bar named Venus in Santiago, Chile. There are now many versions, but this recipe is for the original classic.

daiquiri

SERVES 1

4–6 cracked ice cubes
6 tbsp/2 measures white rum
2 tbsp/3/4 measure lime juice
1/2 tsp sugar syrup

Put the cracked ice cubes into a cocktail shaker and pour in the rum, lime juice, and sugar syrup.

Shake the ingredients vigorously until a frost forms and strain into a chilled cocktail glass.

Party Tip— Make your own party streamers using crepe paper or tissue paper and yarn. Cut strips of paper in various lengths and tie together at one end with the yarn. These are great for hanging in doorways!

This flamboyant cocktail is synonymous with Pat O'Brien's Bar in the New Orleans French Quarter—a popular drink with the tourists because if you manage to drink it all you could take your glass home.

hurricane

SERVES 1

ice
3 tbsp/1 measure lemon juice
12 tbsp/4 measures dark rum
6 tbsp/2 measures sweet fruit juice (passion fruit and orange are the usual)
soda water
slices of orange and cherries, to decorate

Fill a tall cocktail glass or highball glass with ice.

Pour on the ingredients, stir well, then top up with soda water, and dress with the orange slices and cherries.

Party Tip— It's a good idea to provide additional nonalcoholic drinks about an hour before the party is expected to end.

Themed Parties

Cocktail Party

This has to be the ultimate party-lover party, providing the opportunity to shine as the sophisticated host or hostess. The cocktail party offers the chance to add real sparkle to a special occasion, whether it's an anniversary or a graduation celebration.

Preparation

- Inform guests of any dress-code requirements.
- Keep those drinks chilled while the party's heating up, with a good supply of ice.
- Avoid stressing about running out of clean glasses by hiring enough for the evening.

Decor

- Add a little glamor with silver or gold streamers, fused with creams and whites.
- Elegant and exotic flower arrangements make eye-catching additions to any room.

- Simple white Christmas lights bring a glitzy feel to a room without being excessive.

Subtly sophisticated, short and sweet, traditional early evening cocktail parties are a great way to entertain your friends with minimum hassle.

Music

- In keeping with the air of sophistication, play jazz or swing music to create that refined atmosphere.
- As the cocktails start flowing, don't be scared to improvise with the music and adapt it to the mood.

Menu

- Serve delights such as Miniature Pork Brochettes (page 89) and Bleu Cheese & Walnut Tartlets (page 97), on large elegant platters or trays, dressed with sprigs of fresh herbs.
- Why not hire smart professionals to circulate with trays of canapés and cocktails? The effect is well worth it.
- No credible cocktail party would be complete without classics such as the Cosmopolitan (page 102) and the Mimosa (page 105).

Cocktail Know-how

- The standard "measure" used in classic cocktail recipes is a "jigger," which holds 1½ fl oz/45 ml or 3 tablespoons. Of course, it is the proportions that are important, so any small glass can serve as a measure.
- Tasteful garnishes and decorations are a must!

This dip can be served warm or at room temperature. For a lighter snack, serve superior chips, French toast, or bagel chips for dipping.

eggplant & bell pepper dip

SERVES 6–8

2 large eggplants
2 red bell peppers
4 tbsp Spanish olive oil
2 garlic cloves, coarsely chopped
grated rind and juice of 1/2 lemon
1 tbsp chopped fresh cilantro, plus extra sprigs to garnish
1/2–1 tsp paprika
salt and pepper
bread or toast, to serve

Preheat the oven to 375°F/190°C. Prick the skins of the eggplants and bell peppers all over with a fork and brush with about 1 tablespoon of the olive oil. Put on a baking sheet and bake in the oven for 45 minutes, or until the skins are starting to turn black, the flesh of the eggplant is very soft, and the bell peppers are deflated.

When the vegetables are cooked, put them in a bowl and immediately cover tightly with a clean, damp dish towel. Alternatively, you can put the vegetables in a plastic bag. Let them stand for about 15 minutes, until they are cool enough to handle.

When the vegetables have cooled, cut the eggplants in half lengthwise, carefully scoop out the flesh, and discard the skin. Cut the eggplant flesh into large chunks. Remove and discard the stem, core, and seeds from the bell peppers and cut the flesh into large pieces.

Heat the remaining olive oil in a large, heavy-bottom skillet, add the eggplant flesh and bell pepper pieces, and cook for 5 minutes. Add the garlic and cook for an additional 30 seconds.

Turn all the contents of the skillet onto paper towels to drain, then transfer to a food processor. Add the lemon rind and juice, the chopped cilantro, paprika, and salt and pepper to taste, and blend until a speckled purée is formed.

Turn the eggplant and bell pepper dip into a serving bowl. Serve warm, at room temperature, or let cool for 30 minutes, then let chill in the refrigerator for at least 1 hour and serve cold. Garnish with cilantro sprigs and accompany with thick slices of bread or toast for dipping.

The ras-el-hanout spice blend, found in Middle Eastern grocery stores, consists of galangal, rosebuds, black peppercorns, ginger, cardamom, nigella, cayenne, allspice, lavender, cinnamon, cassia, coriander, mace, nutmeg, and cloves!

miniature pork brochettes

MAKES 12

1 lb/450 g lean boneless pork

3 tbsp Spanish olive oil, plus extra for oiling (optional)

grated rind and juice of 1 large lemon

2 garlic cloves, crushed

2 tbsp chopped fresh flat-leaf parsley, plus extra to garnish

1 tbsp ras-el-hanout spice blend

salt and pepper

The brochettes are marinated overnight, so remember to do this in advance so that they are ready when you need them. Cut the pork into pieces about ³/₄ inch/2 cm square and put in a large, shallow, nonmetallic dish that will hold the pieces in a single layer.

To prepare the marinade, put all the remaining ingredients in a bowl and mix well together. Pour the marinade over the pork and toss the meat in it until well coated. Cover the dish and let marinate in the refrigerator for 8 hours or overnight, stirring the pork 2 to 3 times.

You can use wooden or metal skewers to cook the brochettes and for this recipe you will need twelve 6-inch/15-cm skewers. If you are using wooden ones, soak them in cold water for about 30 minutes prior to using. This helps to prevent them from burning and the food sticking to them during cooking. Metal skewers simply need to be greased, and flat ones should be used rather than round ones to prevent the food on them falling off.

Preheat the broiler or barbecue. Thread 3 marinated pork pieces, leaving a little space between each piece, onto each prepared skewer. Cook the brochettes for 10–15 minutes, or until tender and lightly charred, turning several times and basting with the remaining marinade during cooking. Serve the pork brochettes piping hot, garnished with parsley.

Party Tip— Send written invitations for larger parties, telephone or e-mail for smaller ones. Include the theme of the party (cocktails); the occasion, if any; the date, and the beginning and ending times—cocktail parties generally flow between 6 and 8 p.m.

To prepare ahead, bake the potatoes a day in advance and cut into the individual skins. Brush with olive oil, then cover and chill until ready to use.

potato skins with dips

Makes 24

6 large baking potatoes, about 9 oz/250g each, well scrubbed and dried

for the cheese & beer dip
14 oz/400 g sharp Cheddar cheese, grated
1 small garlic clove, crushed
9 fl oz/250 ml lager
1 tsp dry mustard
pinch of cayenne pepper
1 celery stalk, finely chopped

for the bacon & sour cream dip
6 strips bacon, rinds removed, if necessary
10 oz/300 g sour cream
1 bunch scallions, finely chopped
4 tbsp finely snipped fresh chives

Preheat the oven to 425°F/220°C. Place the potatoes directly on the oven rack and bake for 45 minutes–1 hour until very soft and tender when squeezed; remove from the oven and set aside to cool.

Meanwhile, to make the cheese and beer dip, put the cheese, garlic, lager, mustard, and cayenne into a food processor and process. Taste and adjust the seasoning, then spoon into a bowl and stir in the celery. Cover and chill until ready to use.

To make the bacon and sour cream dip, preheat the broiler. Place the bacon on the broiler pan and broil until well cooked and crisp, turning over once. Transfer to crumpled paper towels to drain and leave to cool. Put the sour cream in a bowl with the scallions and chives. Finely chop the bacon and add it to the bowl and stir together. Transfer to a serving bowl, cover and chill until required.

When the potatoes are cool enough to handle, cut them in half lengthwise and then into quarters to make 24 pieces in total. Use a spoon to scoop away the center of the potatoes, leaving a shell about ¹/₂-inch/1-cm thick. Place the potato skins on a baking sheet and lightly brush with oil. Place under the broiler and broil for 10–12 minutes until crisp and lightly brown.

Serve the potato skins hot or warm, with the chilled dips.

This is an elegant alternative to smoked salmon sandwiches. The blinis are delicious freshly cooked, but they can be made up to 2 days in advance and stored in an airtight container. Larger supermarkets often sell ready-made blinis.

smoked salmon blinis

MAKES 24

3 oz/85 g crème fraîche
finely grated rind of
2 lemons
3 tbsp very finely snipped
fresh chives, plus extra
to garnish
pepper
2 oz/55 g smoked salmon,
very finely sliced

for the blinis
3 oz/85 g all-purpose flour
1 tsp active dry yeast
1/2 tsp sugar
5 fl oz/150 ml warm water
3 oz/85 g buckwheat flour
4 fl oz/125 ml warm milk
1 1/2 oz/40 g butter, melted
and cooled
1 large egg, separated
salt and pepper
vegetable oil, for cooking

To make the blinis, stir the all-purpose flour, yeast, and sugar together in a bowl. Make a well in the center and slowly add the water, drawing in flour from the side to make a wet, lumpy batter. Beat until the batter is smooth, then stir in the buckwheat flour, cover the bowl tightly with a kitchen towel, and set aside for 1 hour, until the batter has risen and the surface is covered with air bubbles.

Meanwhile, mix the crème fraîche with the lemon rind, chives, and pepper to taste. Cover and chill until ready to use.

Stir the milk, butter, and egg yolk together with a generous pinch of salt and pepper, then add to the batter, stirring well until blended. Beat the egg white in a separate bowl until soft peaks form, and then fold into the batter.

Heat a large frying pan over medium heat until you can feel the heat rising, then lightly brush the surface all over with vegetable oil using a crumpled paper towel. Fill a tablespoon measure two-thirds full with the batter, then drop the batter onto the hot surface so it forms a circle about 2 inches/5 cm across; add as many more as will fit in the pan without touching. Cook for just over a minute, or until the top surface is covered with air holes and the bottom is golden brown and set. Use a palette knife to flip over the blinis and cook until set and golden brown. Transfer to a heatproof plate and keep warm in a low oven while you cook the remaining batter.

To serve, arrange the warm, not hot, blinis on a platter and top each with about 2 teaspoons of the chilled crème fraîche. Lay the salmon strips over the crème fraîche, add a little piece of chive to each, and serve.

Party Tip—Arrange a few lighthearted party games to help break the ice and encourage guests to mingle.

Potato wedges are an irresistible snack that will be devoured rapidly at any party. The best potato wedges are full of flavor, crisp on the outside, and soft and velvety on the inside. Here, they combine with crispy salmon in a totally superior alternative to fish and chips.

salmon sticks with potato wedges

SERVES 2–3

scant 1 cup fine cornmeal

1 tsp paprika

14 oz/400 g salmon fillet, skinned and sliced into 12 chunky strips

1 egg, beaten

corn oil, for frying

salt and pepper

for the potato wedges

1 lb 2 oz/500 g potatoes, scrubbed and cut into thick wedges

1–2 tbsp olive oil

1/2 tsp paprika

salt

Preheat the oven to 400°F/200°C. To make the potato wedges, dry the potatoes on a clean kitchen towel. Spoon the oil into a roasting pan and put into the preheated oven briefly to heat. Toss the potatoes in the warm oil until well coated. Sprinkle with paprika and salt to taste and roast for 30 minutes, turning halfway through, until crisp and golden.

Meanwhile, mix the cornmeal and paprika together on a plate. Dip each salmon strip into the beaten egg, then roll in the cornmeal mixture until evenly coated.

Pour enough oil into a heavy-bottom frying pan to cover the base and place over a medium heat. When hot, carefully arrange half the salmon strips in the skillet and cook for 6 minutes, turning halfway through, until golden. Drain on paper towels and keep warm while you cook the remaining salmon strips. Serve with the potato wedges.

These tartlets are the ultimate in sophisticated finger food —your guests will be impressed!

bleu cheese & walnut tartlets

MAKES 12

for the walnut pie dough
7 tbsp butter, chilled and diced, plus extra for greasing

scant 1⅝ cups all-purpose flour, plus extra for dusting

pinch of celery salt

¼ cup walnut halves, chopped

for the filling
2 tbsp butter

2 celery stalks, finely chopped

1 small leek, finely chopped

scant 1 cup heavy cream, plus 2 tbsp

7 oz/200 g bleu cheese

salt and pepper

3 egg yolks

chopped fresh flat-leaf parsley and parsley sprigs, to garnish

Lightly grease a 3-inch/7.5-cm 12-hole muffin pan. Sift the flour and celery salt together into a food processor, add the butter, and process until the mixture resembles fine breadcrumbs. Alternatively, rub the fat into the flour mixture in a bowl with your fingertips. Transfer to a large bowl and add the walnuts and enough iced water to form a firm dough.

Turn out onto a lightly floured counter and cut the dough in half. Roll out one half. Using a 3-½ inch/9-cm pastry cutter, cut out 6 circles. Roll out each round to 4½-inch/12-cm in diameter and use to line half the muffin holes. Repeat with the remaining dough. Line each tartlet case with parchment paper and fill with baking beans. Let chill in the refrigerator for 30 minutes. Preheat the oven to 400°F/200°C.

Bake the tartlet cases in the preheated oven for 10 minutes. Remove from the oven, then remove the paper and beans and place on a wire rack to cool.

To make the filling, melt the butter in a skillet over medium–low heat. Add the celery and leek and cook, stirring occasionally, for 15 minutes until very soft. Add 2 tablespoons cream, crumble in the cheese, and mix well. Season to taste with salt and pepper. Put the remaining cream in a pan and bring to a simmer. Place the egg yolks in a heatproof bowl and pour on the cream, stirring constantly. Mix in the cheese mixture and spoon into the tartlet shells.

Bake for 10 minutes, then turn the pan around and bake for an additional 5 minutes. Let the tartlets cool in the pan for 5 minutes. Serve garnished with parsley.

*Party Tip—*Stock up on plenty of ice for chilling wine or champagne as well as serving drinks on the rocks. A good rule of thumb is to provide 1 lb/450 g/2 cups ice per guest.

These are just as meringues should be—as light as air and at the same time crisp and melt-in-the-mouth.

meringues

MAKES 13

4 egg whites
pinch of salt
1/2 cup granulated sugar
1/2 cup superfine sugar
1 1/4 cups heavy cream,
lightly whipped

Preheat the oven to 250°F/120°C. Line 3 cookie sheets with parchment paper.

Using a handheld electric mixer or balloon whisk, beat the egg whites and salt together in a large, clean bowl until stiff—you should be able to turn the bowl upside down without the egg whites falling out.

Whisk in the granulated sugar, a little at a time—the meringue should start to look glossy at this stage. Sprinkle in the superfine sugar, a little at a time, and continue whisking until all the sugar has been incorporated and the meringue is thick, white, and stands in tall peaks.

Transfer the meringue mixture to a pastry bag fitted with a 3/4-inch/2-cm star tip. Pipe 26 small swirls onto the prepared cookie sheets.

Bake in the preheated oven for 1 1/2 hours, or until the meringues are pale golden in color and can be easily lifted off the paper. Turn off the oven and leave the meringues inside overnight.

Just before serving, sandwich the meringues together in pairs with the whipped cream and arrange on a serving plate.

These pretty little cupcakes are perfect for serving at a cocktail party. Look for mini paper cases in specialized cake decoration stores.

tiny chocolate cupcakes

MAKES 20

4 tbsp butter, softened
1/4 cup superfine sugar
1 large egg, lightly beaten
scant 1/2 cup white self-rising flour
2 tbsp unsweetened cocoa
1 tbsp milk
20 chocolate-coated coffee beans, to garnish (optional)

for the chocolate cream
3 1/2 oz/100 g semisweet chocolate
1/3 cup heavy cream

Preheat the oven to 375°F/190°C. Put 20 double-layer mini paper cases on 2 baking sheets.

Put the butter and sugar in a bowl and beat together until light and fluffy. Gradually beat in the egg. Sift in the flour and cocoa and then, using a metal spoon, fold them into the mixture. Stir in the milk.

Fill a pastry bag, fitted with a large plain tip, with the batter and pipe it into the paper cases, half-filling each one.

Bake the cakes in the preheated oven for 10–15 minutes, or until well risen and firm to the touch. Transfer to a wire rack to cool.

To make the chocolate cream, break the chocolate into a pan and add the cream. Heat gently, stirring all the time, until the chocolate has melted. Pour into a large heatproof bowl and, using a handheld electric mixer, beat the mixture for 10 minutes, or until thick, glossy, and cool.

Fill a pastry bag fitted with a large star tip, with the chocolate cream and pipe a swirl on top of each cupcake. Alternatively, spoon the chocolate cream over the top of each cupcake. Chill in the refrigerator for 1 hour before serving. Serve decorated with a chocolate-coated coffee bean, if using.

*Party Tip—*Not everyone will be familiar with cocktail etiquette, so produce a signature cocktail list, designed to match the decorations and invitations. Include ingredients and mixing instructions, then laminate it and pin on the wall near the drinks.

Inviting and refreshing, the Cosmopolitan is the beverage of choice for the "Sex and the City" girls, and is a must at an elegant black-tie affair.

cosmopolitan

SERVES 1

4–6 cracked ice cubes
2 measures vodka
1/2 measure Cointreau
1 measure cranberry juice
juice of 1/2 lime, to garnish
twists of lemon and lime
rind, to garnish

Put the cracked ice cubes into a cocktail shaker. Pour the vodka, Cointreau, and cranberry juice over the ice. Add the lime juice and shake well, then strain into a cocktail glass.

Garnish with a twist of lime rind and a twist of lemon rind.

Party Tip— When planning a cocktail party, it's a good idea to decide on two or three—four at the most—complementary cocktails, rather than having an "open bar" with everyone mixing different (and increasingly weird!) ingredients.

The mimosa is probably the best-known champagne cocktail, traditionally served at brunch, but bubbly enough to impress at a cocktail party.

mimosa

SERVES 1

juice of 1 passion fruit
1/2 measure orange curaçao
crushed ice
champagne, chilled
slice of star fruit and twist
of peel, to garnish

Scoop out the passion fruit flesh into a shaker and shake with the curaçao and a little crushed ice until frosted.

Pour into the base of a champagne glass and top up with champagne. Garnish with a slice of star fruit and a twist of lemon peel.

Party Tip—Remove larger pieces of furniture from the room in which you plan to hold the party. Set up two large tables—one for drinks, the other for food—a good distance from each other, or at opposite ends of the room, to cut down on congestion around them and encourage movement.

Spa Party

Relaxation, indulgence, pampering, and luxury—just what every party-girl needs! The spa party is a great twist on the usual girlie gatherings, perfect for a truly special bachelorette party or memorable baby shower.

Preparation

- Make certain the event won't be disturbed. Enlist the aid of a babysitter if necessary and take that phone off the hook—after all this is supposed to be a stress-free gathering!
- Clear away as much clutter as possible; think minimal and streamline.
- Provide lots of clean fluffy towels to avoid excess mess once all those mud masks are applied.

Decor

- Think soothing and serene with calming colors, such as blue and turquoise.

A home spa party is a fun, different kind of a get-together. And what better way to show your friends how much you appreciate them?

- Lighting can really make a difference here; set the scene with warm and subtle lighting. Try some scented candles with a hint of lavender.

Music

- Soothing sounds are essential to set the tone of the gathering, but remember to keep the volume low to enhance the peaceful ambience.
- Try investing in some meditation, relaxation, or classical music to de-stress.

Menu

- The nutritious and delicious recipes in this chapter will promote a sense of well-being as you pamper your guests and yourself from the outside and inside. Make sure all the ingredients are as fresh as possible and try to find organic options where you can.
- Hydration is the key to any spa. Add variety by serving delicious Fruit Smoothies (page 128) alongside tall glasses of water flavored with detoxifying lemon.

When buying fresh produce, choose artichokes that are dark green, heavy, and have "tight" leaves. Don't select any that are dry-looking or appear to be turning brown.

chicken with linguine & artichokes

SERVES 4

4 chicken breasts, skinned

finely grated rind and juice of 1 lemon

2 tbsp olive oil

2 garlic cloves, crushed

14 oz/400 g canned artichoke hearts, drained and sliced

9 oz/250 g baby plum tomatoes

10½ oz/300 g dried linguine

chopped fresh parsley, to serve

Parmesan cheese, finely grated, to serve

Put each chicken breast between 2 pieces of plastic wrap and bash with a rolling pin to flatten. Put the chicken into a shallow, nonmetallic dish with the lemon rind and juice and 1 tablespoon of the oil and turn to coat in the marinade. Cover and let marinate in the refrigerator for 30 minutes.

Put a large pan of water on to boil. Heat the remaining oil in a skillet over low heat, add the garlic, and cook for 1 minute, stirring frequently. Add the artichokes and tomatoes and cook for 5 minutes, stirring occasionally. Add about half the marinade from the chicken and cook over medium heat for an additional 5 minutes. Cook the linguine in the boiling water for 7–9 minutes, or until just tender.

Meanwhile, preheat the broiler to high. Remove the chicken from the remaining marinade and arrange on the broiler pan. Cook the chicken under the preheated broiler for 5 minutes each side, until thoroughly cooked.

Drain the pasta and return to the pan, pour over the artichoke and tomato mixture, and slice in the cooked chicken.

Divide among 4 warmed serving plates and sprinkle over the parsley and cheese.

Party Tip—Set up stations in your home where your guests can give themselves and each other manicures, pedicures, and facials. Provide each guest with a small foot tub and hand bowl for soaking.

These are an excellent vegetarian choice. They can be served hot or at room temperature. If you make them in advance for serving cold, be sure to remove them from the refrigerator 30 minutes before serving.

Catalan stuffed bell peppers

MAKES 8 HALVES

10 oz/300 g baby spinach leaves, rinsed

2 tbsp olive oil

1 small onion, finely chopped

2 large garlic cloves, crushed

1/4 tsp ground turmeric

large pinch of ground cinnamon

large pinch of cayenne pepper, or to taste

4 tbsp pine nuts, toasted

4 tbsp raisins

10 oz/250 g basmati rice, rinsed until the water runs clear and soaked in water to cover for at least 30 minutes

salt and pepper

4 large bell peppers, assorted colors, halved

Put the spinach in a large pan with just the water clinging to the leaves, cover, and cook over medium heat until it has wilted. Drain well, and when cool enough to handle squeeze out all the water. Chop finely and set aside.

Meanwhile, preheat the oven to 350°F/180°C. Heat 1 tablespoon of the oil in a large skillet over medium heat. Add the onion and cook for 5 minutes or until soft. Add the garlic, turmeric, cinnamon and cayenne pepper and cook for 2 minutes.

Stir in the pine nuts, raisins, and drained rice. Add the chopped spinach and stir together then season with salt and pepper to taste; set aside.

Cut each pepper in half lengthwise, and then carefully remove the cores and seeds. Take care not to cut away the stem ends. You should have a deep container for stuffing. Divide the rice stuffing equally among the pepper halves, and then arrange them in 1 or 2 large flameproof containers (such as roasting pans) that support them tightly.

Bake in the preheated oven for 45 minutes–1 hour and serve immediately.

Prepare the food for the skewers by making sure it's trimmed properly and bite-sized. The longer the food takes to cook, the less suitable it is for skewering.

broiled tuna & vegetable kabobs

SERVES 4

4 tuna steaks, about
5 oz/140 g each

2 red onions

12 cherry tomatoes

1 red bell pepper, seeded
and diced into 1-inch/
2.5-cm pieces

1 yellow bell pepper, seeded
and diced into 1-inch/
2.5-cm pieces

1 zucchini, sliced

1 tbsp chopped fresh
oregano

4 tbsp olive oil

freshly ground black pepper

1 lime, cut into wedges,
to serve

Preheat the broiler to high. Cut the tuna into 1-inch/2.5-cm pieces. Peel the onions, leaving the root intact, and cut each onion lengthwise into 6 wedges.

Divide the fish and vegetables evenly among 8 wooden skewers (presoaked to avoid burning) and arrange on the broiler pan.

Mix the oregano and oil together in a small bowl. Season to taste with pepper. Lightly brush the kabobs with the oil and cook under the preheated broiler for 10–15 minutes or until evenly cooked, turning occasionally. If you cannot fit all the kabobs on the broiler pan at once, cook them in batches, keeping the cooked kabobs warm while you cook the remainder. Alternatively, these kabobs can be cooked on a barbecue.

Garnish with lime wedges and serve with a selection of salads, cooked couscous, new potatoes, or bread.

Party Tip—Serve sparkling water or juice in pretty glasses with lemon, lime, or orange slices. Food should be nutritious—fruits and vegetables are the ideal choice.

When correctly cooked, the texture of couscous is light and fluffy. It should not be gummy or gritty.

couscous salad with roasted butternut squash

SERVES 2

2 tbsp honey

4 tbsp olive oil

1 butternut squash, peeled, seeded, and cut into 3/4-inch/2-cm chunks

1¼ cups couscous

1¾ cups low-salt vegetable stock

½ cucumber, diced

1 zucchini, diced

1 red bell pepper, seeded and diced

juice of ½ lemon

sea salt and pepper

2 tbsp chopped fresh parsley

Preheat the oven to 375°F/190°C. Mix half the honey with 1 tablespoon of the oil in a large bowl, add the squash, and toss well to coat. Transfer to a roasting pan and roast in the preheated oven for 30–40 minutes until soft and golden.

Meanwhile, put the couscous in a heatproof bowl. Heat the stock in a pan and pour over the couscous, cover, and leave for 3 minutes. Add 1 tablespoon of the remaining oil and fork through, then stir in the diced cucumber, zucchini, and red bell pepper. Re-cover and keep warm.

Whisk the remaining honey and oil with the lemon juice in a pitcher and season to taste with salt and pepper. Stir the mixture through the couscous.

To serve, top the couscous with the roasted squash and sprinkle with the parsley.

Party Tip— When compiling your guest list, it's a good idea to keep numbers smaller for a more intimate party to make sure that everyone has room to relax and enjoy the day or evening. Encourage your guests to wear comfortable clothing; you could even ask them to bring slippers and a bathrobe.

Portobellos are large brown cup-shaped or flat-shaped mushrooms, depending on the stage at which they are picked. Freshly picked portobellos are sweet, juicy, and flavorsome.

baked mushrooms

SERVES 4

2 tbsp olive oil

8 portobello mushrooms

2 oz/55 g white mushrooms, finely chopped

2 garlic cloves, crushed

4 slices lean cooked ham, finely chopped

2 tbsp finely chopped fresh parsley

pepper

4 slices rye bread, to serve

Preheat the oven to 375°F/190°C. Brush a baking sheet with a little of the oil. Arrange the portobello mushrooms, cup side up, on the baking sheet.

Mix the white mushrooms, garlic, ham, and parsley together in a bowl.

Divide the ham mixture among the portobello mushroom cups. Drizzle with the remaining oil and season to taste with pepper.

Bake in the preheated oven for 10 minutes, then serve immediately with rye bread.

Party Tip—Create a soothing atmosphere with soft lighting, scented candles, and relaxing music. Clear as much space as possible in your living room and be sure the bathroom is sparkling clean. Provide lots of fluffy towels and pillows.

Look for eggplants that are plump and firm, with unblemished, glossy skin and bright color.

eggplant tagine with polenta

SERVES 2

1 eggplant, cut into
1/2-inch/1-cm cubes

3 tbsp olive oil

1 large onion, thinly sliced

1 carrot, diced

2 garlic cloves, chopped

4 oz/115 g brown-cap
mushrooms, sliced

2 tsp ground coriander

2 tsp cumin seeds

1 tsp chili powder

1 tsp ground turmeric

2 1/2 cups canned chopped
tomatoes

1 1/4 cups vegetable stock

1 tbsp tomato paste

scant 1/2 cup plumped dried
apricots, coarsely chopped

14 oz/400 g canned
chickpeas, drained and
rinsed

2 tbsp fresh cilantro,
to garnish

for the cornmeal

5 cups hot vegetable stock

1/4 cup instant cornmeal

salt and pepper

Preheat the broiler to medium. Toss the eggplant in 1 tablespoon of the oil and arrange in the broiler pan. Cook under the preheated broiler for 20 minutes, turning occasionally, until softened and starting to blacken around the edges—brush with more oil if the eggplant becomes too dry.

Heat the remaining oil in a large, heavy-bottom pan over medium heat. Add the onion and cook, stirring occasionally, for 8 minutes, or until soft and golden. Add the carrot, garlic, and mushrooms and cook for 5 minutes. Add the spices and cook, stirring constantly, for an additional minute.

Add the tomatoes and stock, stir well, then add the tomato paste. Bring to a boil, then reduce the heat and let simmer for 10 minutes, or until the sauce starts to thicken and reduce.

Add the eggplant, apricots, and chickpeas, partially cover, and cook for an additional 10 minutes, stirring occasionally.

Meanwhile, to make the cornmeal, pour the hot stock into a nonstick pan and bring to a boil. Pour in the cornmeal in a steady stream, stirring constantly with a wooden spoon. Reduce the heat to low and cook for 1–2 minutes, or until the cornmeal thickens to a mashed potato-like consistency. Serve the tagine with the cornmeal, sprinkled with the fresh cilantro.

Warming cinnamon smells fabulous with aromatic orange. Prepare the fruit in advance, place in a dish, cover, and chill. Sprinkle with cinnamon before serving.

broiled cinnamon oranges

SERVES 4

4 large oranges
1 tsp ground cinnamon
1 tbsp raw brown sugar

Preheat the broiler to high. Cut the oranges in half and discard any pits. Using a sharp or curved grapefruit knife, carefully cut the flesh away from the skin by cutting around the edge of the fruit. Cut across the segments to loosen the flesh into bite-size pieces that will spoon out easily.

Place the orange halves, cut side up, in a shallow, heatproof dish. Mix the cinnamon with the sugar in a small bowl and sprinkle evenly over the orange halves. Cook under the preheated broiler for 3–5 minutes, or until the sugar has caramelized and is golden and bubbling. Serve immediately.

Party Tip—Fresh fruit makes superb face packs. Go "au naturel" by crushing three large strawberries per person and apply, washing off with rosewater. Or, try a mashed creamy avocado face pack, and rinse with cold water.

Even spa parties need something a little sweet. These carrot bars are bursting with taste and goodness.

carrot bars

MAKES 14–16 BARS

sunflower oil, for oiling
6 oz/175 g unsalted butter
1/2 cup brown sugar
2 eggs, beaten
scant 1/2 cup self-rising whole-wheat flour, sifted
1 tsp baking powder, sifted
1 tsp ground cinnamon, sifted
1 1/8 cups ground almonds
4 oz/115 g carrot, coarsely grated
1/2 cup golden raisins
1/2 cup plumped dried apricots, finely chopped
scant 3/8 cup toasted chopped hazelnuts
1 tbsp slivered almonds

Preheat the oven to 350°F/180°C. Lightly oil a 10 x 8-inch/25 x 20-cm shallow, rectangular baking pan and line with parchment paper.

Cream the butter and sugar together in a bowl until light and fluffy, then gradually beat in the eggs, adding a little of the flour after each addition.

Add all the remaining ingredients, except the slivered almonds. Spoon the mixture into the prepared pan and smooth the top. Sprinkle with the slivered almonds.

Bake in the preheated oven for 35–45 minutes, or until the mixture is cooked and a skewer inserted into the center comes out clean.

Remove from the oven and let cool in the pan. Remove from the pan, discard the parchment paper, and cut into bars.

Treat your guests to these delicious, light, and healthy alternatives to store-bought ice cream. They look very impressive but are simple to make.

apricot & yogurt cups

SERVES 12

2¹/2 cups plain yogurt
few drops of almond extract
2–3 tsp honey, warmed
scant ¹/2 cup whole blanched almonds
1 cup plumped dried apricots

Line a 12-cup muffin pan with small paper cake cases.

Spoon the yogurt into a mixing bowl, add the almond extract and honey, and stir well. Using a small, sharp knife, cut the almonds into very thin slivers and stir into the yogurt mixture. Using a pair of kitchen scissors, cut the apricots into small pieces, then stir into the yogurt.

Spoon the mixture into the paper cases and freeze for 1¹/2–2 hours, or until just frozen. Serve at once.

Party Tip—Think about hiring health and beauty practitioners who make home visits. They will take care of all the supplies, and each guest can pay for their beauty treatments—so you don't have to worry about a thing!

Melon contains high levels of vitamin C, which is necessary for blood-sugar control—it can also help strengthen arteries.

melon & ginger sorbet

SERVES 4

1 ripe melon, peeled, seeded, and cut into chunks

juice of 2 limes

1 tbsp grated fresh ginger

4 tbsp unrefined superfine sugar

1 egg white, lightly whisked

fresh strawberries or raspberries, to serve

Put the melon, lime juice, and ginger into a food processor or blender and process until smooth. Pour into a measuring cup and make up to 2½ cups with cold water.

Pour into a bowl and stir in the sugar. Beat in the egg white. Transfer to a freezerproof container and freeze for 6 hours. Serve in scoops with strawberries or raspberries.

*Party Tip—*In keeping with the spa atmosphere, you might want to have lots of upscale fashion magazines on hand to keep guests entertained while they wait for their nails to dry!

For the ultimate in healthy indulgence, spoil your guests with a selection of homemade real fruit smoothies.

fruit smoothies

cherry sour
SERVES 2
9 oz/250 g bottled Morello cherries
2/3 cup strained plain yogurt
sugar, to taste
almond cookies, to serve
fresh cherries on a toothpick, to garnish

kiwi cooler
SERVES 2
4 ripe kiwis, peeled and cut into fourths
3/4 cup sparkling lemonade
2 large scoops ice cream or sherbet

mango & orange smoothie
SERVES 2
1 large ripe mango
juice of 2 medium oranges
3 scoops mango sherbet
1 strip orange zest, to garnish

honeydew smoothie
SERVES 2
9 oz/250 g honeydew melon
1 1/4 cups sparkling mineral water
2 tbsp clear honey

To make the cherry sour, make sure that you use the bottling liquid as well as the fruit. Put the cherries with their bottling liquid into a blender with the yogurt and sugar to taste and process until smooth. Pour into glasses and garnish with cherries on a toothpick.

To make the kiwi cooler, put the kiwis and lemonade into a blender and process until smooth. Pour into glasses and top with a scoop of ice cream or sherbet. You can use either strawberry ice cream, to contrast with the green of the smoothie, or a lime sherbet to blend in with it. Serve at once.

To make the mango & orange smoothie, cut the mango lengthwise through the flesh as close to the large flat central pit as possible. Turn the mango over and do the same on the other side of the pit. Remove the peel and roughly chop the flesh before placing in a blender. Add the orange juice and sherbet and process until smooth. If you want a creamier smoothie, use vanilla ice cream instead of mango sherbet. Pour into glasses and serve at once, decorated with a strip of orange peel.

To make the honeydew smoothie, cut the rind off the melon and chop the flesh into chunks, discarding any seeds. Put the melon into a blender with the water and honey, and process until smooth. Pour into glasses and serve immediately.

Brunch Party

What better way to really show your nearest and dearest what they mean to you than a gathering dedicated to them? Perfect for any family occasion, whether it's Mother's Day, Father's Day, or simply a chance to say thank you for all the support they give you, the brunch party will be appreciated and remembered.

Preparation

- Arrange a day when everyone is available. Sundays can often be the best option as people are less likely to have other commitments.
- Be prepared to keep children amused by organizing games and activities.

Decor

- Aim for a relaxed, comfortable, and inviting atmosphere.
- Clear away any breakable items if young children are coming.

A leisurely weekend brunch is a perfect way to relax and entertain family and friends.

- Create a relaxing space for the adults, away from the children's games and activities—giving parents the chance to savor a saucy Bloody Mary cocktail! (page 151)

Music

- Try to avoid conflict over music tastes and opt for neutral, mellow music at a low, background volume that will satisfy everyone.
- If in doubt, ask people to bring along some of their favorite lazy-day songs.

Menu

- These versatile and varied dishes are an exciting alternative to the usual fried foods, and will definitely keep everyone satisfied for hours after the meal.
- Choose dishes that can be made in advance, such as delicious Mini Bacon & Egg Pastries with Cheddar (page 132), or a speedy spread, like Scrambled Eggs with Smoked Salmon (page 136).
- Simple menus will go down best with the family, so maybe try the easy yet traditional Apple Pancakes with Maple Syrup Butter (page 143).

Take care not to force the dough circles into the muffin pans as stretched dough will shrink during baking.

mini bacon & egg pastries with cheddar

MAKES 12

butter, for greasing
1 lb 2 oz/500 g prepared pie dough
all-purpose flour, for rolling
2 tbsp whole-grain mustard
12 lean bacon slices, diced, cooked, and drained well
12 small eggs
pepper
1 cup grated Cheddar cheese
2 tbsp chopped fresh parsley

Preheat the oven to 350°F/180°C. Lightly grease a deep 12-cup muffin pan.

Roll the dough out to a 1/4-inch/5-mm thickness on a lightly floured counter and cut out 12 circles, approximately 5 inches/13 cm in diameter. Use to line the cups of the muffin pan, gently pleating the sides of the dough as you ease it into the molds. Place 1/2 teaspoon mustard into the base of each pastry shell and top with a little of the bacon.

Break an egg into a cup, spoon the yolk into the pastry shell, then add enough of the white to fill the pastry shell about two-thirds full. Do not overfill. Season to taste with pepper and sprinkle the grated cheese evenly over the tops of the pastries. Bake for 20–25 minutes, or until the egg is set and the cheese is golden brown. Serve warm, sprinkled with chopped parsley.

Party Tip— If you are planning a brunch party for Mother's Day, arrange it all so that Mom doesn't need to lift a finger and can sit back and enjoy a well-earned day off!

For best results when poaching eggs, break them into a cup first, then slide them into the hot water. Poach for a little longer than the suggested 3 minutes if you prefer firmer yolks.

eggs benedict with quick hollandaise sauce

SERVES 4

1 tbsp white wine vinegar
4 eggs
4 English muffins
4 slices good-quality ham

for the quick hollandise sauce
3 egg yolks
7 oz/200 g butter
1 tbsp lemon juice
pepper

Fill a wide skillet three-quarters full with water and bring to a boil over low heat. Reduce the heat to a simmer and add the vinegar. When the water is barely simmering, carefully break each egg into a cup, then slide them into the pan, one at a time. Let stand for 1 minute, then, using a large spoon, gently loosen the eggs from the bottom of the skillet. Let cook for an additional 3 minutes, or until the white is cooked and the yolk is still soft, basting the top of the egg with the water from time to time.

Meanwhile, to make the hollandaise sauce, place the egg yolks in a blender or food processor. Melt the butter in a small pan until bubbling. With the motor running, gradually add the hot butter to the egg yolks in a steady stream, blending until the sauce is thick and creamy. Add the lemon juice, and a little warm water if the sauce is too thick, then season to taste with pepper. Remove from the blender or food processor and keep warm.

Split the muffins and toast them on both sides. To serve, top each muffin with a slice of ham, a poached egg, and a generous spoonful of hollandaise sauce.

As a variation, try using smoked trout and snipped chives, or even fresh crabmeat as a substitute—delicious!

scrambled eggs with smoked salmon

SERVES 4

8 eggs

1/3 cup light cream

2 tbsp chopped fresh dill, plus extra, to garnish

salt and pepper

3 1/2 oz/100 g smoked salmon, cut into small pieces

2 tbsp butter

8 slices of rustic bread, toasted

Break the eggs into a large bowl and whisk together with the cream and dill. Season to taste with salt and pepper. Add the smoked salmon and mix to combine.

Melt the butter in a large nonstick skillet and pour in the egg and smoked salmon mixture. Using a wooden spatula, gently scrape the egg away from the sides of the skillet as it starts to set and swirl the skillet slightly to allow the uncooked egg to fill the surface.

When the eggs are almost cooked but still creamy, remove from the heat and spoon onto the prepared toast. Serve immediately, garnished with a sprig of dill.

Party Tip—To create the mood for the party, set the table with pretty flatware, folded napkins, and fresh flowers. Add vanilla or lavender scented candles if you don't use flowers.

When selecting asparagus, look for straight green, rounded stalks of a similar size so that they cook uniformly. Avoid asparagus with woody spears or any with a particularly strong odor.

asparagus with poached eggs & parmesan

SERVES 4

10½ oz/300 g asparagus, trimmed
1 tbsp white wine vinegar
4 large eggs
3 oz/85 g Parmesan cheese
pepper

Bring 2 skillets of water to a boil. Add the asparagus to 1 skillet, return to a simmer, and cook for 5 minutes, or until just tender.

Meanwhile, reduce the heat of the second skillet to a simmer and add the vinegar. When the water is barely simmering, carefully break each egg into a cup, then slide them into the skillet, one at a time. Leave for 1 minute, then using a large spoon, gently loosen the eggs from the bottom of the skillet. Leave to cook for an additional 3 minutes, or until the white is cooked and the yolk is still soft, basting the top of the eggs with the water from time to time. Remove with a slotted spoon.

Drain the asparagus and divide among 4 warmed plates. Top each plate of asparagus with an egg and shave over the cheese. Season to taste with pepper and serve immediately.

Use firm but ripe bananas for this recipe, as softer bananas may disintegrate too easily. Try pears or strawberries for a delicious alternative.

waffles with caramelized bananas

MAKES 12

scant 1¼ cups all-purpose flour

2 tsp baking powder

½ tsp salt

2 tsp superfine sugar

2 eggs, separated

1 cup milk

3 oz/85 g butter, melted

for the caramelized bananas

3½ oz/100 g butter, cut into pieces

3 tbsp corn syrup

3 large ripe bananas, peeled and thickly sliced

Mix the flour, baking powder, salt, and sugar together in a bowl. Whisk the egg yolks, milk, and melted butter together with a fork, then stir this mixture into the dry ingredients to make a smooth batter.

Using a handheld electric mixer, beat the egg whites in a clean glass bowl until stiff peaks form. Fold into the batter mixture. Spoon 2 large tablespoons of the batter into a preheated waffle maker and cook according to the manufacturer's instructions.

To make the caramelized bananas, melt the butter with the corn syrup in a pan over low heat and stir until combined. Let simmer for a few minutes until the caramel thickens and darkens slightly. Add the bananas and mix gently to coat. Pour over the warm waffles and serve at once.

Party Tip—Do as much preparation as you can the day before. Many recipes can be prepared the day before and cooked on the day or finished the night before and served cold.

As the batter sits, it tends to thicken up and can make the pancakes fairly heavy. If the mixture becomes too thick while you are cooking the pancakes, add a little extra milk before continuing.

apple pancakes with maple syrup butter

MAKES 18

scant 1½ cups self-rising flour
½ cup superfine sugar
1 tsp ground cinnamon
1 egg
scant 1 cup milk
2 apples, peeled and grated, plus wedges, to garnish
1 tsp butter

for the maple syrup butter
3 oz/85 g butter, softened
3 tbsp maple syrup

Mix the flour, sugar, and cinnamon together in a bowl and make a well in the center. Beat the egg and the milk and pour into the well. Using a wooden spoon, gently incorporate the dry ingredients into the liquid until well combined, then stir in the grated apple.

Heat the butter in a large nonstick skillet over low heat until melted and bubbling. Add tablespoons of the pancake mixture to form 3½-inch/9-cm circles. Cook each pancake for about 1 minute, until it starts to bubble lightly on the top and looks set, then flip it over and cook the other side for 30 seconds, or until cooked through. The pancakes should be golden brown; if not, increase the heat a little. Remove from the skillet and keep warm. Repeat the process until all of the pancake batter has been used up (it is not necessary to add extra butter).

To make the maple syrup butter, melt the butter with the maple syrup in a pan over low heat and stir until combined. To serve, place the pancakes on serving dishes and spoon over the flavored butter. Serve warm, garnished with apple wedges.

Start this recipe the night before. Make the dough and roll out the croissants, then brush with the glaze, cover with plastic wrap, and refrigerate overnight. The next morning, let rise for 30–45 minutes, then proceed as per the recipe.

fresh croissants

MAKES 12

1 lb 2 oz/500 g white bread flour, plus extra for rolling

scant ¼ cup superfine sugar

1 tsp salt

2 tsp active dry yeast

1¼ cups milk, heated until just warm to the touch

10½ oz/300 g butter, softened, plus extra for greasing

1 egg, lightly beaten with 1 tbsp milk, for glazing

Preheat the oven to 400°F/200°C. Stir the dry ingredients into a large bowl, make a well in the center, and add the milk. Mix to a soft dough, adding more milk if too dry. Knead on a lightly floured counter for 5–10 minutes, or until smooth and elastic. Let rise in a large greased bowl, covered, in a warm place until doubled in size. Meanwhile, flatten the butter with a rolling pin between 2 sheets of waxed paper to form a rectangle about ¼-inch/5-mm thick, then let chill.

Knead the dough for 1 minute. Remove the butter from the refrigerator and let soften slightly. Roll out the dough on a well floured counter to 18 x 6 inches/45 x 15 cm. Place the butter in the center, folding up the sides and squeezing the edges together gently. With the short end of the dough toward you, fold the top third down toward the center, then fold the bottom third up. Rotate 90° clockwise so that the fold is to your left and the top flap toward your right. Roll out to a rectangle and fold again. If the butter feels soft, wrap the dough in plastic wrap, and let chill. Repeat the rolling process twice more. Cut the dough in half. Roll out one half into a triangle ¼-inch/ 5-mm thick (keep the other half refrigerated). Use a cardboard triangular template, base 7 inches/18 cm and sides 8 inches/20 cm, to cut out the croissants.

Brush the triangles lightly with the glaze. Roll into croissant shapes, starting at the base and tucking the point underneath to prevent the croissants from unrolling while cooking. Brush again with the glaze. Place on an ungreased baking sheet and let double in size. Bake for 15–20 minutes until golden brown.

Party Tip—Families love to pitch in. If you'd appreciate the help, then say so. If, however, there are too many cooks in your kitchen, calmly and cheerfully ban them from your creative area!

The banana bread can be stored in the freezer for up to 3 months. Thaw overnight in the refrigerator before serving. The bread can also be frosted for a delicious dessert.

banana bread with strawberry compote

SERVES 8

4¹/2 oz/125 g butter, softened, plus extra for greasing
¹/2 cup superfine sugar
¹/4 cup brown sugar
3 eggs
1 tsp vanilla extract
3 large ripe bananas
scant 2 cups self–rising flour
1 tsp freshly grated nutmeg
1 tsp ground cinnamon

for the strawberry compote
scant ¹/2 cup brown sugar
juice of 2 oranges
grated rind of 1 orange
1 cinnamon stick
2¹/2 cups strawberries, thickly sliced
mascarpone or plain yogurt, to serve
confectioners' sugar, sifted, for dusting

Preheat the oven to 350°F/180°C. Grease a 9 x 4¹/4-inch/23 x 11-cm loaf pan and line the bottom with parchment paper.

Place the butter and sugars in a bowl and beat together until light and fluffy. Add the eggs, one at a time, then mix in the vanilla extract. Peel the bananas and mash coarsely with the back of a fork. Stir gently into the butter mixture, then add the flour, nutmeg, and cinnamon, stirring until just combined.

Pour the mixture into the prepared pan and bake for 1 hour 15 minutes, or until a skewer inserted into the center comes out free of sticky mixture. Remove from the oven and let stand for 5 minutes before turning out onto a wire rack.

To make the compote, mix the brown sugar, orange juice, orange rind, and cinnamon stick together in a medium pan and bring to a boil. Add the strawberries and return to a boil. Remove from the heat, pour into a clean heatproof bowl, and let cool. Serve slices of the banana bread with a dollop of mascarpone or yogurt and spoon over the warm or cold compote. Dust with sifted confectioners' sugar.

This is the perfect drink to serve at a family gathering and, being just a little different, it will instantly boost your status as host or hostess.

mint julep

SERVES 1

leaves from 1 fresh mint sprig
1 tbsp sugar syrup
crushed ice cubes
3 measures bourbon whiskey
fresh mint sprig, to garnish

Put the mint leaves and sugar syrup into a small chilled glass and mash with a teaspoon.

Add crushed ice to fill the tumbler, then add the bourbon. Garnish with the mint sprig.

Party Tip—Stock up on a selection of gourmet teas and coffees. Superb Chinese and Ayurvedic teas are available, and rich organic coffees will radiate a wonderful welcoming smell.

Nothing's better in the morning than the tomato, spice, and chili flavor combination of a Bloody Mary.

bloody mary

SERVES 1

dash of Worcestershire sauce
dash of Tabasco sauce
cracked ice cubes
2 measures vodka
splash dry sherry
6 measures tomato juice
juice of ½ lemon
pinch celery salt
pinch cayenne pepper
celery stalk with leaves,
to garnish
slice of lemon, to garnish

Dash the Worcestershire sauce and Tabasco sauce over ice in a shaker and add the vodka, splash of dry sherry, tomato juice, and lemon juice.

Shake vigorously until frosted.

Strain into a tall chilled glass, add a pinch of celery salt and a pinch of cayenne and garnish with the celery stalk and the slice of lemon.

Party Tip—Find out beforehand if any of your guests are vegetarian. If they are, clearly label dishes as vegetarian if it is not immediately obvious.

Parties for All Seasons

Barbecue Party

The sunshine is finally here so take advantage of those balmy summer evenings and plan a stylish barbecue party. Barbecues don't need to be messy affairs with second-rate food—this chapter shows how to set the standard.

Preparation

• The barbecue party really has to be one of the easiest to prepare, so you can take advantage of those scorching summer days on impulse.

• Don't forget, however, to make sure you know how many meat-eaters and vegetarians to cater for.

Decor

• Make sure that your garden or yard looks the part by distributing pots of seasonal flowers.

• Clean patio furniture and a tidy outdoor eating area are important, so get brushing, mowing, and weeding!

Make the most of your patio. Have a selection of windbreaks, a gazebo, and garden umbrellas to ensure optimum comfort.

- To have no furniture is a better option than having people sit on broken plastic chairs.
- Picnic blankets spread around create an informal atmosphere and people can relax and chat on the lawn.
- Invest in some outdoor lighting so the party can continue even when the daylight doesn't.

Music

- Classic summer songs are a must-have for this affair.
- Don't forget that while you may be soaking up the sunshine, the neighbors may not be so appreciative, so try to keep the music to a reasonable level.

Menu

- Be creative with your barbecue and try less traditional fare, such as Chargrilled Tuna with Chili Salsa (page 167).
- Don't forget about any vegetarian guests; offer them the tempting Three-Bean Burgers with Green Mayo (page 163).
- Keep everyone refreshed and cool, even when the temperatures soar, with a good supply of Raspberry & Apple Quencher (page 172) poured over ice.

Coated in a spicy marinade and served with a colorful, chargrilled pepper sauce, these delicious chicken wings are perfect as part of a summer barbecue lunch party.

spicy chicken wings

SERVES 4

16 chicken wings
4 tbsp corn oil
4 tbsp light soy sauce
2-inch/5-cm piece of fresh ginger, coarsely chopped
2 garlic cloves, coarsely chopped
grated rind and juice of 1 lemon
2 tsp ground cinnamon
2 tsp ground turmeric
4 tbsp honey
salt and pepper

for the sauce
2 orange bell peppers
2 yellow bell peppers
corn oil, for brushing
1/2 cup plain yogurt
2 tbsp dark soy sauce
2 tbsp chopped fresh cilantro

Place the chicken wings in a large, shallow, nonmetallic dish. Put the oil, soy sauce, ginger, garlic, lemon rind and juice, cinnamon, turmeric, and honey into a food processor and process to a smooth purée. Season to taste with salt and pepper. Spoon the mixture over the chicken wings and turn until thoroughly coated. Cover with plastic wrap and let marinate in the refrigerator for up to 8 hours.

Preheat the barbecue. To make the sauce, brush the bell peppers with the oil and cook over hot coals, turning frequently, for 10 minutes, or until the skin is blackened and charred. Remove from the barbecue and let cool slightly, then remove the skins and discard the stem and the seeds. Put the flesh into a food processor with the yogurt and process to a smooth purée. Transfer to a bowl and stir in the soy sauce and chopped cilantro.

Drain the chicken wings, reserving the marinade. Cook over medium-hot coals, turning and brushing frequently with the reserved marinade, for 8–10 minutes, or until thoroughly cooked. Serve immediately with the sauce.

No barbecue is complete without the classic hamburger. The patties are seasoned with onion, garlic, and mustard, but you can make them in the pure tradition of steak, salt, and pepper, if you wish.

the classic hamburger (with fried onions)

SERVES 4–6

1 lb/450 g lean rump steak or top round, freshly ground
1 onion, grated
2–4 garlic cloves, crushed
2 tsp whole-grain mustard
pepper

for the fried onions
2 tbsp olive oil
1 lb/450 g onions, finely sliced
2 tsp brown sugar
burger buns or soft rolls, to serve

Place the ground steak, onion, garlic, mustard, and pepper in a large bowl and mix together thoroughly, squeezing the meat with your hands. Shape into 4–6 equal-size burgers, then cover and let chill for 30 minutes.

Meanwhile, heat the oil in a heavy-bottom skillet. Add the onions and sauté over low heat until soft. Add the sugar and cook for an additional 8 minutes, stirring occasionally, or until the onions have caramelized. Drain well on paper towels and keep warm.

To cook the burgers on the barbecue, check that they are very firm and brush generously with oil. Cook for about 5 minutes on each side. Split the buns for serving and toast them, cut sides down, on the barbecue. Serve the burgers in the buns with the onions.

Party Tip—Remember to cook vegetarian food on a separate grill from meat and fish as the meat could spit and get onto the vegetables if cooked nearby.

You can prepare this dish with any kind of individual lamb pieces—leg chops or cutlets are especially tender but quite small, in which case you will probably require 2 per serving. Shoulder steaks also work well.

lamb chops with mint

SERVES 4

6 chump chops, about
6 oz/175 g each

2/3 cup strained plain yogurt

2 garlic cloves,
finely chopped

1 tsp grated fresh ginger

1/4 tsp coriander seeds,
crushed

salt and pepper

1 tbsp olive oil, plus extra
for brushing

1 tbsp orange juice

1 tsp walnut oil

2 tbsp chopped fresh mint

Place the chops in a large, shallow, nonmetallic bowl. Mix half the yogurt, the garlic, ginger, and coriander seeds together in a measuring cup and season to taste with salt and pepper. Spoon the mixture over the chops, turning to coat, then cover with plastic wrap and let marinate in the refrigerator for 2 hours, turning occasionally.

Preheat the barbecue. Place the remaining yogurt, the olive oil, orange juice, walnut oil, and mint in a small bowl, and whisk until thoroughly blended. Season to taste with salt and pepper. Cover the minted yogurt with plastic wrap and let chill in the refrigerator until ready to serve.

Drain the chops, scraping off the marinade. Brush with olive oil and cook over medium-hot coals for 5–7 minutes on each side. Serve immediately with the minted yogurt.

Party Tip—Sprinkle the coals with herbs such as rosemary, sage, and mint while you are cooking. This produces a delightful fragrance and imparts flavor to the food.

If you are feeling adventurous, try using a hotter variety of fresh chile in the burgers, such as habañero or pequín chiles. Remember to seed them before use.

three-bean burgers with green mayo

SERVES 4–6

10½ oz/300 g canned cannellini beans, drained

10½ oz/300 g canned black-eyed peas, drained

10½ oz/300 g canned red kidney beans, drained and rinsed

1 fresh chile, seeded

4 shallots, cut into quarters

2 celery stalks, coarsely chopped

1 cup fresh whole-wheat breadcrumbs

1 tbsp chopped fresh cilantro

salt and pepper

2 tbsp whole-wheat flour

2 tbsp corn oil

4 burger buns or soft rolls, to serve

2 yellow, red, or green bell peppers (or mixed), seeded and thinly sliced, to serve

salad greens, to serve

for the green mayo

6 tbsp mayonnaise

2 tbsp chopped fresh parsley or mint

1 tbsp chopped cucumber

3 scallions, finely chopped

Place all the beans, chile, shallots, celery, breadcrumbs, cilantro, and salt and pepper to taste in a food processor and, using the pulse button, blend together. Shape into 4–6 equal-size burgers, then cover and let chill for 1 hour. Coat the burgers lightly in the flour.

Preheat the barbecue. To make the green mayo, place the mayonnaise, parsley, cucumber, and scallions in a bowl and mix together. Cover and chill until ready to serve.

To cook the burgers on the barbecue, check that they are very firm and brush generously with oil. Cook for about 5 minutes on each side.

Split and toast the buns or rolls on the barbecue. Place pepper strips and salad greens on the bottom halves of the buns. Add the burgers and top with the green mayo. Replace the bun top and serve.

The delicious cheese flavor in this recipe is sure to make these sausages a hit with everyone, whether vegetarian or not. They are great for enlivening your barbecue menu.

vegetarian sausages

SERVES 4

1 tbsp corn oil, plus extra for oiling

1 small onion, finely chopped

1¾ oz/50 g mushrooms, finely chopped

½ red bell pepper, seeded and finely chopped

14 oz/400 g canned cannellini beans, rinsed and drained

2 cups fresh breadcrumbs

1 cup grated Cheddar cheese

1 tsp dried mixed herbs

1 egg yolk

seasoned all-purpose flour

small bread rolls, fried onion slices, and tomato chutney, to serve

Heat the corn oil in a pan. Add the onion, mushrooms, and bell pepper, and cook until softened.

Mash the cannellini beans in a large bowl. Add the onion, mushroom, and bell pepper mixture, and the breadcrumbs, cheese, herbs and egg yolk and mix well. Press the mixture together with your fingers and shape into 8 sausages. Roll each sausage in the seasoned flour. Chill in the refrigerator for at least 30 minutes.

Preheat the barbecue. Cook the sausages on a sheet of oiled aluminum foil set over medium-hot coals for 15–20 minutes, turning and basting frequently with oil, until golden. Split the bread rolls down the center and insert a layer of cooked onions. Place the sausages in the rolls and serve with tomato chutney.

Party Tip— Finger bowls are essential for cleaning sticky fingers. Fill several small glass bowls with warm water and add thin slices of lemon or rose petals.

Tuna steaks are a perfect candidate for barbecuing. They are firm and easy to turn, and here the colorful and spicy chili salsa keeps them moist and full of flavor.

chargrilled tuna with chili salsa

SERVES 4

4 tuna steaks,
about 6 oz/175 g each

grated rind and juice of
1 lime

2 tbsp olive oil

salt and pepper

fresh cilantro sprigs,
to garnish

for the chili salsa

2 orange bell peppers

1 tbsp olive oil

juice of 1 lime

juice of 1 orange

2–3 fresh red chiles,
seeded and chopped

pinch of cayenne pepper

salt and pepper

Rinse the tuna thoroughly under cold running water and pat dry with paper towels, then place in a large, shallow, nonmetallic dish. Sprinkle the lime rind and juice and the olive oil over the fish. Season to taste with salt and pepper, cover with plastic wrap, and let marinate in the refrigerator for up to 1 hour.

Preheat the barbecue. To make the salsa, brush the bell peppers with the olive oil and cook over hot coals, turning frequently, for 10 minutes, or until the skin is blackened and charred. Remove from the barbecue and let cool slightly, then remove the skins and discard the seeds. Put the bell peppers into a food processor with the remaining salsa ingredients and process to a purée. Transfer to a bowl and season to taste with salt and pepper.

Cook the tuna over hot coals for 4–5 minutes on each side, until golden. Transfer to serving plates, garnish with cilantro sprigs, and serve with the salsa.

At the end of the barbecue, when the coals have virtually died, whole bananas can be grilled straight on them, skins intact.

chocolate rum bananas

SERVES 4

1 tbsp butter
8 oz/225 g semisweet or
milk chocolate
4 large bananas
2 tbsp rum
sour cream, mascarpone
cheese, or ice cream, and
grated nutmeg, to serve

Take four 10-inch/25-cm squares of aluminum foil and brush them with butter.

Cut the chocolate into very small pieces. Make a careful slit lengthwise in the peel of each banana, and open just wide enough to insert the chocolate. Place the chocolate pieces inside the bananas, along their lengths, then close them up.

Wrap each stuffed banana in a square of foil, then barbecue them over hot coals for about 5–10 minutes, or until the chocolate has melted inside the bananas. Remove from the barbecue, place the bananas on individual serving plates, and pour some rum into each banana.

Serve at once with sour cream, mascarpone cheese, or ice cream, topped with nutmeg.

*Party Tip—*Marshmallows are old favorites for rounding off your barbecue. Toast by holding them over the coals on long-handled metal toasting forks or long metal skewers, protecting fingers with folded napkins.

There is nothing quite like the unique taste and texture of fresh figs—lusciously sweet, they are an ideal treat for any barbecue party.

stuffed figs

SERVES 4

8 fresh figs
3¹/2 oz/100 g cream cheese
1 tsp ground cinnamon
3 tbsp brown sugar
sprigs of fresh mint,
to garnish

Cut out eight 7-inch/18-cm squares of aluminum foil. Make a small slit in each fig, then place each fig on a square of foil.

Put the cream cheese in a bowl. Add the cinnamon and stir until well combined. Stuff the inside of each fig with the cinnamon cream cheese, then sprinkle about a teaspoon of sugar over each one. Close the foil around each fig to make a package.

Place the packages on the barbecue and cook over hot coals, turning them frequently, for about 10 minutes, or until the figs are cooked to your taste. Transfer the figs to serving plates and garnish with fresh mint.

Barbecues can be thirsty work, and this refreshing and tangy drink is perfect for everyone.

raspberry & apple quencher

SERVES 2

8 ice cubes, crushed
2 tbsp raspberry syrup
2¼ cups chilled apple juice
whole raspberries, apple pieces, to garnish

Divide the crushed ice between the glasses and pour over the raspberry syrup.

Top up each glass with chilled apple juice and stir well. Garnish with the whole raspberries and pieces of apple speared on toothpicks and serve.

*Party Tip—*Do as much preparation as you can the day before your party. Make the marinades, and if appropriate, marinate the meat or poultry. Fish requires only about 20–30 minutes marinating time before cooking.

This traditional Cuban cocktail has returned to being in vogue. Impress your guests with this refreshing, revitalizing, and delicious treat!

club mojito

SERVES 6

1 tsp sugar syrup
a few mint leaves, plus more to garnish
juice of 1/2 lime
ice
6 tbsp/2 measures Jamaican rum
soda water
dash of Angostura bitters

Put the syrup, mint leaves, and lime juice in a highball glass. Crush the mint leaves and add to the glass.

Add ice and rum, then top up with soda water to taste.

Finish with a dash of Angostura bitters and a mint leaf.

*Party Tip—*Cooking in foil is ideal for foods that can easily fall apart, stick, or burn, like fish. Tear off a sheet of foil and brush with oil before adding the fish, skin side down. Season with salt and pepper, a squeeze of lemon, and an optional splash of white wine. Seal the corners of the foil and barbecue for about 3 minutes on each side.

Garden Party

The garden party is the perfect opportunity to enjoy preparing and sharing a stylish summer spread. With the right menu and decor, and some fine weather, everyone could be relaxing anywhere in the world.

Preparation

- As the aim is to convey an air of elegance, make certain that your garden is as polished as your culinary offerings.
- Be prepared for unpredictable rainfall with a contingency plan, such as a small marquee or drinks in the conservatory.

Decor

- Simple and stylish is the way to go. Complement your groomed garden with clean white linen and an uncluttered table arrangement.

Summer is the easiest season for entertaining as nature does the decorating for you and seasonal produce is abundant and inexpensive.

- Tasteful lanterns and garden candles will create a chic climate and allow the cultured conversation to continue late into the evening.
- Insect-repellent candles should be placed around the area—perhaps on side tables—but not on the main table as the scent may overpower the food and drink.

Music

- Think of all those heavenly evenings on vacation in exotic places sampling local cuisines and take your musical inspiration from sunny places. For example, try Italian classics and central American salsa.

Menu

- The elegant and effortless recipes in this chapter will really make you feel like you are taking a vacation from the normal culinary chores.
- Serve sumptuous Salmon & Avocado Salad (page 182) on large, stylish white plates to emphasize the crisp colors of the cuisine.
- Alfresco dining would not be complete without a constant supply of Gin Sling (page 198), laden with lots of fresh fruit.

Arugula has become a fashionable salad vegetable in many homes and restaurants, but it has never been out of favor in Italy where it grows wild.

prosciutto with arugula

SERVES 4

4 oz/115 g arugula
1 tbsp lemon juice
salt and pepper
3 tbsp extra-virgin olive oil
8 oz/225 g prosciutto,
sliced thinly

Separate the arugula leaves, wash in cold water, and pat dry on paper towels. Place the leaves in a bowl.

Pour the lemon juice into a small bowl and season to taste with salt and pepper. Whisk in the olive oil, then pour the dressing over the arugula leaves and toss lightly so they are evenly coated.

Carefully drape the prosciutto in folds on 4 individual serving plates, then add the arugula. Serve at room temperature.

Party Tip— Use lavish candles for after-dark dining. They can be set in tall glasses, hurricane candle-holders, or small colored glass vases.

Dried cherries or other dried fruits can be used instead of the cranberries.

smoked chicken & cranberry salad

SERVES 4

1 smoked chicken, weighing
3 lb/1.3 kg

scant 1 cup dried cranberries

2 tbsp apple juice or water

7 oz/200 g sugar snap peas

2 ripe avocados

juice of 1/2 lemon

4 lettuce hearts

1 bunch of watercress,
trimmed

2 oz/55 g arugula

1/2 cup walnuts, chopped,
to garnish (optional)

for the dressing

2 tbsp olive oil

1 tbsp walnut oil

2 tbsp lemon juice

1 tbsp chopped fresh mixed
herbs, such as parsley and
lemon thyme

salt and pepper

Carve the chicken carefully, slicing the white meat. Divide the legs into thighs and drumsticks and trim the wings. Cover with plastic wrap and refrigerate.

Put the cranberries in a bowl. Stir in the apple juice, then cover with plastic wrap and let soak for 30 minutes.

Meanwhile, blanch the sugar snap peas, then refresh under cold running water and drain.

Peel, pit, and slice the avocados, and toss in the lemon juice to prevent browning.

Separate the lettuce hearts and arrange on a large serving platter with the avocados, sugar snap peas, watercress, arugula, and chicken.

Put all the dressing ingredients, with salt and pepper to taste, in a screw-top jar, then screw on the lid and shake until well blended.

Drain the cranberries and mix them with the dressing, then pour over the salad.

Serve immediately, scattered with walnuts, if using.

Fresh fish should never smell fishy. The flesh should be bright and moist and never discolored at the edges.

salmon & avocado salad

SERVES 4

1 lb/450 g new potatoes

4 salmon steaks, about 4 oz/115 g each

1 avocado

juice of 1/2 lemon

1 1/4 cups baby spinach leaves

4 1/2 oz/125 g mixed small salad greens, including watercress

12 cherry tomatoes, halved

scant 1/2 cup chopped walnuts

for the dressing

3 tbsp unsweetened clear apple juice

1 tsp balsamic vinegar

freshly ground black pepper

Cut the new potatoes into bite-size pieces, put into a pan, and cover with cold water. Bring to a boil, then reduce the heat, cover, and let simmer for 10–15 minutes, or until just tender. Drain and keep warm.

Meanwhile, preheat the broiler to medium. Cook the salmon steaks under the preheated broiler for 10–15 minutes, depending on the thickness of the steaks, turning halfway through cooking. Remove from the broiler and keep warm.

While the potatoes and salmon are cooking, cut the avocado in half, remove and discard the pit, and peel the flesh. Cut the avocado flesh into slices and coat in the lemon juice to prevent it from discoloring.

Toss the spinach and mixed greens together in a bowl. Add the cherry tomato halves and avocado. Arrange the salad on 4 individual plates.

Remove and discard the skin and any bones from the salmon. Flake the salmon and divide among the plates along with the potatoes. Sprinkle the walnuts over the salads.

To make the dressing, mix the apple juice and vinegar together in a small bowl or pitcher and season well with pepper. Drizzle over the salads and serve immediately.

Party Tip—Provide your guests with options for escaping from the sun. Whether it's a gazebo, chairs placed under a shady tree, or tables with umbrellas, your guests will appreciate somewhere to escape from the heat.

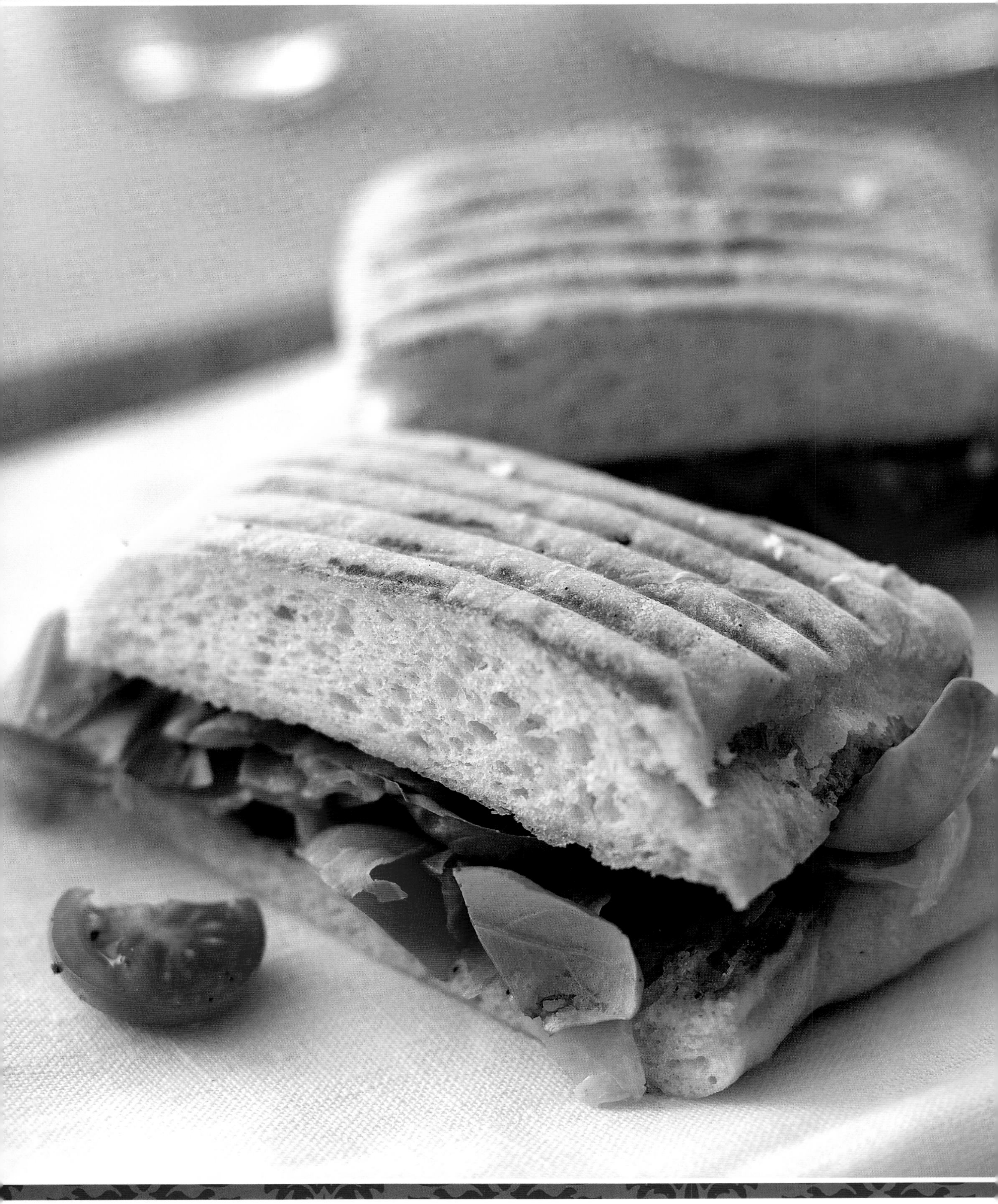

For a vegetarian version, omit the prosciutto and cover the tomatoes with thin slices of goat cheese.

ciabatta sandwiches

MAKES 4

2 loaves ciabatta bread, each cut in half
extra-virgin olive oil
salt and pepper
about 8 oz/225 g cherry tomatoes, cut in half
8 thin slices prosciutto
1 small bunch fresh basil leaves

Using a serrated knife, cut each loaf of bread in half through the center horizontally, then brush the cut sides with olive oil. Sprinkle the bottom halves with salt and pepper to taste, then divide the tomato halves among the bottom pieces of bread, cut sides down.

Top each sandwich base with 2 slices of prosciutto, folded to fit as necessary, then add fresh basil leaves. Place the tops on the sandwiches and press down, crushing the tomatoes into the bread.

Preheat a sandwich toaster or griddle and brush the bread with a little oil. Toast the sandwiches lightly, to brown and crisp the crust, turning them once if cooking on a griddle. Serve.

Party Tip—Use as many fresh, seasonal ingredients in your menu as possible. As thirsts increase during the summer, appetites for heavy recipes shrink. Opt for salads and grilled or broiled foods, which you'll find much quicker and cooler to prepare in the hot weather.

In Greece, grape leaves are picked when they are young and tender and are used to wrap small parcels of savory rice as well as whole fish.

stuffed grape leaves

MAKES ABOUT 30

8 oz/225 g package grape leaves preserved in brine

2/3 cup arborio or other short-grain rice

salt and pepper

3/4 cup olive oil

1 small onion, chopped finely

1 garlic clove, chopped finely

1/3 cup pine nuts, chopped

1/3 cup currants

3 scallions, chopped finely

1 tbsp chopped fresh mint

1 tbsp chopped fresh dill

2 tbsp chopped fresh flat-leaf parsley

juice of 1 lemon

1/4 pint/50 ml water

lemon wedges, to serve

Place the grape leaves in a large bowl, pour over boiling water, and leave to soak for 20 minutes. Drain, soak in cold water for 20 minutes, and then drain again.

Meanwhile, put the rice and a pinch of salt in a saucepan. Cover with cold water and bring to a boil, then simmer for 15-20 minutes, or as directed on the package, until tender. Drain well, put in a bowl, and set aside to cool.

Heat 2 tablespoons of the oil in a large, heavy-bottomed skillet, add the onion and garlic, and cook for 5-10 minutes until softened. Add the onions to the rice with the pine nuts, currants, scallions, mint, dill, and parsley. Season with a little salt and plenty of pepper and mix the ingredients well together.

Place 1 grape leaf, vein-side upward, on a work surface. Put a little filling on the base of the leaf and fold up the bottom ends of the leaf. Fold the sides of the leaf into the center then roll up the leaf around the filling. Squeeze the packet gently in your hand to seal. Continue filling and rolling the grape leaves until all the ingredients have been used up, putting any torn grape leaves in the bottom of a large flameproof casserole or Dutch oven. Put the stuffed leaves, seam-side down and in a single layer, in the casserole, packing them as close together as possible.

Mix the remaining oil and the lemon juice with 2/3 cup water and pour into the casserole. Place a large plate over the grape leaves to keep them in place, then cover the casserole with a lid. Bring to a simmer and simmer for 45 minutes.

Leave the grape leaves to cool in the liquid. Serve the grape leaves warm or chilled, with lemon wedges.

If you're a successful gardener you may well be feeling overwhelmed by a glut of seasonal vegetables in summer. This recipe is an ideal way of using them and one that everyone will enjoy.

mixed vegetable bruschetta

SERVES 4

olive oil, for brushing
and drizzling
1 red bell pepper, halved
and seeded
1 orange bell pepper, halved
and seeded
4 thick slices baguette or
ciabatta
1 fennel bulb, sliced
1 red onion, sliced
2 zucchini, sliced diagonally
2 garlic cloves, halved
1 tomato, halved
salt and pepper
fresh sage leaves, to garnish

Brush an electric grill with oil and preheat. Cut each bell pepper in half lengthwise into 4 strips. Toast the bread slices on both sides in a toaster or under a broiler.

When the grill is hot add the bell peppers and fennel and cook for 4 minutes, then add the onion and zucchini, and cook for 5 minutes, until all the vegetables are tender but still with a slight "bite." If necessary, cook the vegetables in 2 batches, as they should be placed on the grill in a single layer.

Meanwhile, rub the garlic halves over the toasts, then rub them with the tomato halves. Place on warm plates. Pile the grilled vegetables on top of the toasts, drizzle with olive oil, and season with salt and pepper. Garnish with sage leaves and serve warm.

New potatoes are plentiful during the summer months, so take advantage with this delicious and simple side dish.

buttered new potatoes with herbs

SERVES 4

12 small new potatoes
1/2 cup butter
2 tbsp finely chopped fresh rosemary
salt and pepper

Boil the potatoes in salted water until just tender. Drain well.

Melt the butter in a large, heavy skillet. Add the rosemary and the potatoes and mix well. Continue cooking, stirring frequently, for 5 minutes, or until the potatoes are thoroughly coated in rosemary butter and are starting to brown.

Arrange the potatoes in large bowls, sprinkle with salt and pepper, and serve immediately.

Party Tip— It's worth investing in a couple of stylish but practical garden umbrellas in case of rain. Supply a few snug blankets for ladies in summer dresses and continue the party, dry and happy under the umbrellas!

If you wash the summer fruits just before using them, be sure to drain them well on paper towels, otherwise the liquid will make the pastry cases soggy.

summer fruit tartlets

MAKES 12

for the pastry

1 1/3 cups all-purpose flour, plus extra for dusting

3/4 cup confectioners' sugar

1/2 cup ground almonds

1 stick unsalted butter, diced and chilled

1 egg yolk

1 tbsp milk

for the filling

1 1/2 cups cream cheese

confectioners' sugar, to taste, plus extra for dusting

12 oz/350 g fresh summer berries and currants, such as blueberries, raspberries, small strawberries, red currants, and white currants, picked over and prepared

To make the pastry, sift the flour and sugar into a bowl, then stir in the almonds. Rub in the butter with your fingertips until the mixture resembles breadcrumbs. Add the egg yolk and milk and mix to form a dough. Turn out onto a lightly floured counter and knead briefly. Wrap and chill in the refrigerator for 30 minutes.

Preheat the oven to 400°F/200°C. Roll out the pastry and use it to line 12 deep tartlet or individual brioche pans. Prick the pastry bottoms with a fork. Press a piece of foil into each tartlet, covering the edges, and bake in the preheated oven for 10–15 minutes, or until light golden-brown. Remove the foil and bake for an additional 2–3 minutes. Transfer the pastry shells to a wire rack to cool.

To make the filling, mix the cream cheese and sugar together in a bowl. Put a spoonful of filling in each pastry shell and arrange the fruit on top. Dust with sifted confectioners' sugar and serve immediately.

Other varieties of rippled fruit ice cream, such as raspberry and strawberry, can be made in the same way. Simply replace the blueberries with your chosen fruits.

rippled blueberry ice cream

SERVES 6–8

scant 2 cups whole milk
1 vanilla bean
1¼ cups superfine sugar
4 egg yolks
scant 2 cups fresh blueberries, plus extra to garnish
6 tbsp water
scant 2 cups heavy whipping cream
vanilla ice cream, to serve

Pour the milk into a heavy-bottom pan, add the vanilla bean, and bring almost to a boil. Remove from the heat and let infuse for 30 minutes.

Put scant ²/₃ cup of the sugar and the egg yolks in a large bowl and whisk together until pale and the mixture leaves a trail when the whisk is lifted. Remove the vanilla bean from the milk, then slowly add the milk to the sugar mixture, stirring all the time with a wooden spoon. Strain the mixture into the rinsed-out pan or a double boiler and cook over low heat for 10–15 minutes, stirring all the time, until the mixture thickens enough to coat the back of the spoon. Do not let the mixture boil or it will curdle.

Remove the custard from the heat and chill for at least 1 hour, stirring from time to time to prevent a skin from forming.

Meanwhile, strip the blueberries from their stalks using the tines of a fork and put them in a heavy-bottom pan with the remaining sugar and the water. Heat gently, stirring, until the sugar has dissolved, then let simmer gently for 10 minutes, or until the blueberries are very soft.

Push the blueberries through a nylon strainer into a bowl to remove the seeds, then let the purée cool. Meanwhile, whip the cream until it holds its shape. Keep in the refrigerator until ready to use.

If using an ice-cream machine, fold the cold custard into the whipped cream, then churn the mixture in the machine following the manufacturer's instructions. Just before the ice cream freezes, spread half in a freezerproof container. Pour over half the blueberry purée, then repeat the layers. Freeze for 1–2 hours, or until firm or ready to serve. Alternatively, freeze the custard in a freezerproof container, uncovered, for 1–2 hours, or until it starts to set around the edges. Turn the custard into a bowl and stir with a fork or beat in a food processor until smooth. Fold in the whipped cream. Spread half back into the container, then pour over half the blueberry purée. Repeat the layers. Return to the freezer and freeze for 2–3 hours, or until firm or ready to serve. Cover the container with a lid for storing. Serve garnished with blueberries.

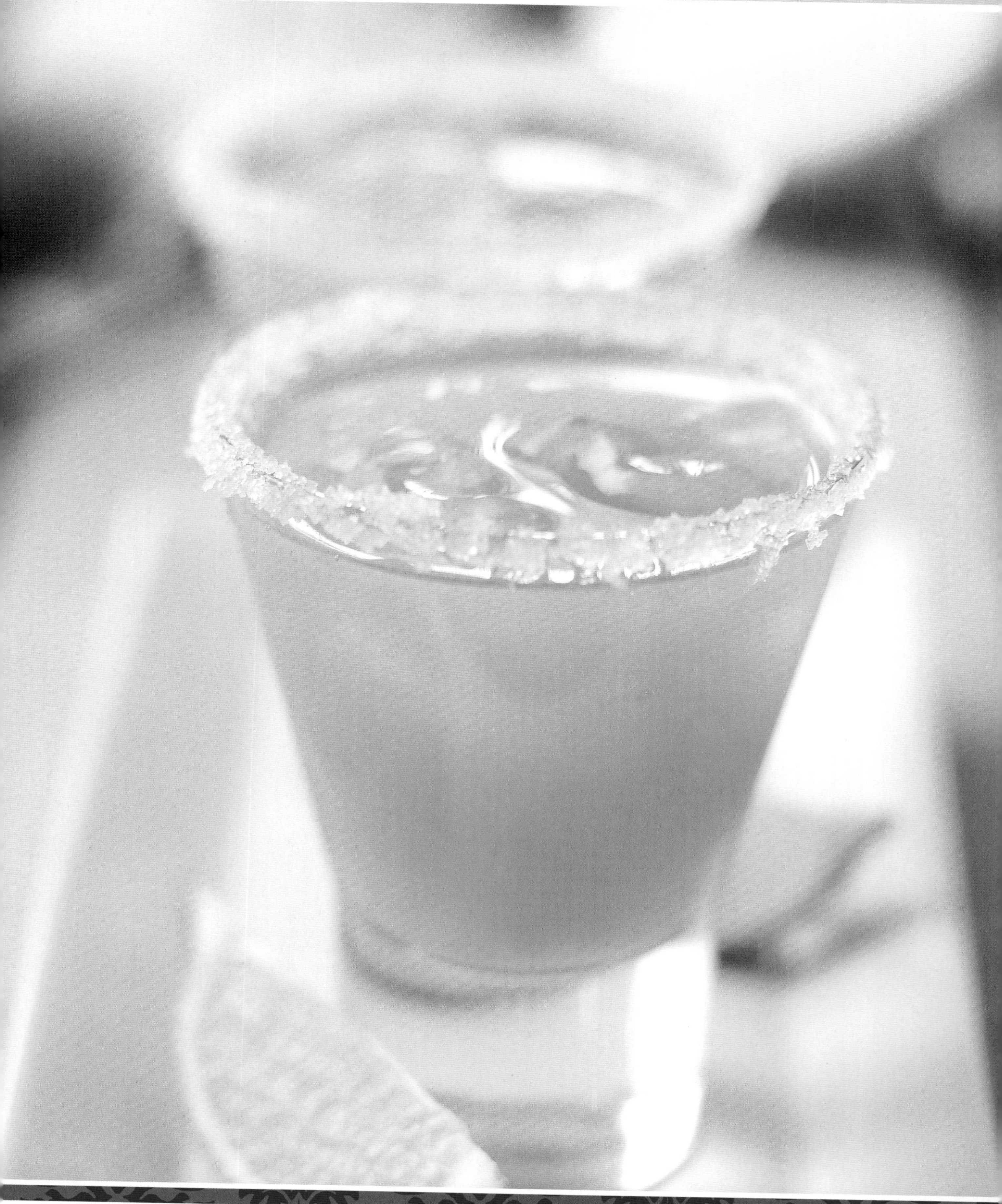

Iced tea is always refreshing and even if you are not a tea drinker, this version is especially fresh and fruity. Keep some in the refrigerator if you don't use it all up.

orange & lime iced tea

SERVES 2

1¼ cups water
2 tea bags
scant ½ cup orange juice
4 tbsp lime juice
1–2 tbsp brown sugar
wedges of lime and
granulated sugar, to serve
8 ice cubes

Pour the water into a pan and bring to a boil. Remove from the heat, add the tea bags, and let stand for 5 minutes to infuse. Remove the tea bags and let the tea cool to room temperature (about 30 minutes). Transfer to a pitcher, cover with plastic wrap, and chill in the refrigerator for at least 45 minutes.

When the tea has chilled, pour in the orange juice and lime juice. Add brown sugar to taste.

Take two glasses and rub the rims with a wedge of lime, then dip them in granulated sugar to frost. Put the ice cubes into the glasses and pour over the tea. Serve with wedges of lime.

Party Tip—From soda and beer to blended drinks, always offer a good choice at summer parties. Include plenty of bottled water on your shopping list, and place buckets filled with ice cubes at various points so guests can help themselves.

Gin Sling is a long, deliciously dry but fruity concoction, with a gin base flavored with herbs. In England, no garden party would be complete without a pitcher of it!

Gin Sling

SERVES 1

6–8 cracked ice cubes
3 tbsp Pimm's No. 1
lemonade, to top up
wedges of cucumber,
sprig of fresh mint and
slices of orange and lemon,
to decorate

Fill a large glass two-thirds full with the cracked ice cubes and pour in Pimm's No. 1. Top up with lemonade and stir gently.

Decorate with wedges of cucumber, a sprig of fresh mint, and slices of orange and lemon.

Party Tip— Be the ultimate party host or hostess by providing personal items your guests may have forgotten such as sun screen or wraps to keep out the evening chill.

Winter Warming Party

With the winter nights drawing in, what better way to keep the cold out than with an evening of hearty food and hospitality? The Winter Warming Party is the perfect excuse to banish those winter blues and warm up for the festive season.

Preparation

- Decide on your guests; is this going to be a cozy family affair or a chance for some festivities with friends?

- Prepare as much food as possible in advance and coordinate cooking times so that you'll be able to concentrate on entertaining your guests.

Nothing beats the feeling of comfort that only a roaring open fire can bring—so why not treat your guests to some hearty, warming food, served in the fireside glow?

Decor

- Create a cozy, comfortable atmosphere with lots of rich fall colors and inviting soft furnishings.

- Soft lighting will bring a warm glow to the occasion. Candles are always a classic option.

- Try some musky scents with incense burners to conjure a welcoming warmth.

- If possible, nothing beats a roaring log-fire to warm those frosty fingers.

Menu

- These wholesome and hearty recipes will put a glow on everyone's cheeks on those frosty winter evenings.

- Allowing people to help themselves to Thick Beef & Pearl Onion Casserole (page 206) and Roasted Root Vegetables (page 210) will ensure everyone is warmed from the inside out.

- An Irish Coffee (page 221) to end the evening will keep the cold out as your guests enjoy the crisp night air.

So simple, so traditional, and so delicious—this soup can be taken into the garden in mugs for an outdoor treat.

winter warmer
red lentil soup

SERVES 4

1 cup red lentils
1 red onion, diced
2 large carrots, sliced
1 celery stalk, sliced
1 parsnip, diced
1 garlic clove, crushed
5 cups vegetable stock
2 tsp paprika
freshly ground black pepper
4 tbsp fromage frais or a
little walnut oil
1 tbsp snipped fresh chives,
to garnish

Put the lentils, onion, vegetables, garlic, stock, and paprika into a large pan. Bring to a boil and boil rapidly for 10 minutes. Reduce the heat, cover, and let simmer for 20 minutes, or until the lentils and vegetables are tender.

Let the soup cool slightly, then purée in small batches in a food processor. Process until the mixture is smooth.

Return the soup to the pan and heat through thoroughly. Season to taste with pepper.

To serve, ladle the soup into warmed bowls or mugs and swirl in a tablespoonful of fromage frais or drizzle with a little walnut oil. Sprinkle the chives over the soup to garnish and serve immediately.

*Party Tip—*If you are planning to hold a fireworks display, why not theme your invitations? Try a simple design with a chic black background and a selection of colorful bursts.

Soups do not come much heartier than this—the perfect winter warmer for your guests.

winter minestrone
with sausage

SERVES 4

3 tbsp olive oil

9 oz/250 g coarse-textured pork sausage, peeled and cut into chunks

1 onion, sliced thinly

2 garlic cloves, chopped very finely

7 oz/200 g canned chopped tomatoes

2 tbsp chopped fresh mixed herbs, such as flat leaf parsley, sage, and marjoram

1 celery stalk, sliced thinly

1 carrot, diced

1 small red bell pepper, seeded and diced

3¾ cups chicken stock

salt and pepper

scant ½ cup short macaroni

½ cup drained canned navy beans

1 cup frozen peas

2 tbsp freshly grated Parmesan, plus extra to serve

4 thick slices Italian bread, to serve

Heat the oil in a large pan over medium–low heat. Add the sausage and onion. Cook, stirring occasionally, until the onion is just colored.

Add the garlic, tomatoes, and herbs. Cook for 5 minutes, stirring. Add the celery, carrot, and bell pepper, cover, and cook the mixture for 5 minutes.

Pour in the stock. Bring to a boil, then cover and simmer gently for 30 minutes.

Season the soup with salt and pepper. Add the macaroni and beans and simmer for about 15 minutes, or until the macaroni is just tender.

Stir in the peas and cook for 5 minutes. Stir in the Parmesan.

To serve, place the bread in individual serving bowls. Ladle the soup over the bread and let stand for a few minutes. Serve with plenty of freshly grated Parmesan.

Serve this straight from the cooking pot, allowing guests to help themselves, and appreciate the rich, satisfying winter warming casserole.

thick beef & pearl onion casserole

SERVES 6

2 tbsp olive oil

1 lb/450 g pearl onions, peeled but kept whole

2 garlic cloves, halved

2 lb/900 g stewing beef, cubed

1/2 tsp ground cinnamon

1 tsp ground cloves

1 tsp ground cumin

2 tbsp tomato paste

salt and pepper

3 cups full-bodied red wine

grated rind and juice of 1 orange

1 bay leaf

1 tbsp chopped fresh flat-leaf parsley, to garnish

boiled or mashed potatoes, to serve

Preheat the oven to 300°F/150°C. Heat the oil in a large, flameproof casserole and cook the whole onions and garlic, stirring frequently, for 5 minutes, or until softened and beginning to brown. Add the beef and cook over high heat, stirring frequently, for 5 minutes, or until browned on all sides.

Stir the spices and tomato paste into the casserole and add salt and pepper to taste. Pour in the wine, scraping any sediment from the bottom of the casserole, then add the orange rind and juice and the bay leaf. Bring to a boil and cover.

Cook in the preheated oven for about 2 hours. Remove the lid and cook the casserole for an additional hour, stirring once or twice, until the meat is tender. Remove from the oven and garnish with the parsley. Serve hot, accompanied by boiled or mashed potatoes.

This melt-in-the-mouth mixture of tomatoes, eggplant, and celery, flavored with garlic and capers, is a traditional Sicilian dish.

warm vegetable medley

SERVES 4

4 tbsp olive oil

2 celery stalks, sliced

2 red onions, sliced

1 lb/450 g eggplant, diced

1 garlic clove, chopped finely

5 plum tomatoes, chopped

3 tbsp red wine vinegar

1 tbsp sugar

3 tbsp green olives, pitted

2 tbsp capers

salt and pepper

4 tbsp chopped fresh
flat-leaf parsley

ciabatta or fresh bread,
to serve

Heat half the olive oil in a large, heavy-bottom pan. Add the celery and onions and cook over low heat, stirring occasionally, for 5 minutes, until softened but not colored. Add the remaining oil and the eggplant. Cook, stirring frequently, for about 5 minutes, until the eggplant starts to color.

Add the garlic, tomatoes, vinegar, and sugar, and mix well. Cover the mixture with a circle of waxed paper and let simmer gently for about 10 minutes.

Remove the waxed paper, stir in the olives and capers, and season to taste with salt and pepper. Pour the mixture into a serving dish and set aside to cool to room temperature. Sprinkle the parsley over the vegetables and serve serve with warm ciabatta or fresh bread.

Root vegetables are winter staples. Roasted root vegetables are particularly popular since they all cook together and need little attention once prepared.

roasted root vegetables

SERVES 4–6

3 parsnips, cut into
2-inch/5-cm chunks

4 baby turnips, quartered

3 carrots, cut into
2-inch/5-cm chunks

1 lb/450 g butternut squash,
peeled and cut into
2-inch/5-cm chunks

1 lb/450 g sweet potatoes,
peeled and cut into
2-inch/5-cm chunks

2 garlic cloves, finely chopped

2 tbsp chopped fresh
rosemary

2 tbsp chopped fresh thyme

2 tsp chopped fresh sage

3 tbsp olive oil

salt and pepper

2 tbsp chopped fresh mixed
herbs, such as parsley,
thyme, and mint, to garnish

Preheat the oven to 425°F/220°C. Arrange all the vegetables in a single layer in a large roasting pan. Sprinkle over the garlic and the herbs. Pour over the oil and season well with salt and pepper. Toss all the ingredients together until they are well mixed and coated with the oil (you can let them marinate at this stage to allow the flavors to be absorbed).

Roast the vegetables at the top of the oven for 50–60 minutes until they are cooked and nicely browned. Turn the vegetables over halfway through the cooking time.

Serve with a good handful of fresh herbs sprinkled on top and a final seasoning of salt and pepper to taste.

Party Tip—As the esteemed host or hostess, do your best to meet and greet all your guests as they arrive—people will appreciate the personal gesture and you can briefly explain the agenda for the evening.

When roasted, garlic loses its pungent acidity and acquires a delicious, full-flavored sweetness. It gives puréed potatoes a delicious party twist!

roasted garlic mashed potatoes

SERVES 4

2 whole garlic bulbs
1 tbsp olive oil
2 lb/900 g starchy potatoes, peeled
salt and pepper
1/2 cup milk
2 oz/55 g butter

Preheat the oven to 350°F/180°C. Separate the garlic cloves, place on a large piece of foil, and drizzle with the oil. Wrap the garlic in the foil and roast in the oven for about 1 hour, or until very tender. Let cool slightly.

About 20 minutes before the end of the cooking time, cut the potatoes into chunks, then cook in a pan of lightly salted boiling water for 15 minutes, or until tender.

Squeeze the cooled garlic cloves out of their skins and push through a strainer into a pan. Add the milk, butter, and salt and pepper to taste and heat gently until the butter has melted.

Drain the cooked potatoes, then mash in the pan until smooth. Pour in the garlic mixture and heat gently, stirring, until the ingredients are combined. Serve hot.

This is an enormously popular contemporary version of the classic French dessert. The recipe is simple to make and certain to impress.

crème brûlée

SERVES 4–6

8–10½ oz mixed soft fruits, such as blueberries and pitted fresh cherries

1½–2 tbsp Cointreau or orange flower water

9 oz/250 g mascarpone cheese

1 cup sour cream

2–3 tbsp dark brown sugar

Prepare the fruit, if necessary, and lightly rinse, then place in the bases of four to six 5-fl oz ramekin dishes. Sprinkle the fruit with the Cointreau or orange flower water.

Cream the cheese in a bowl until soft, then gradually beat in the sour cream.

Spoon the cheese mixture over the fruit, smoothing the surface and making sure that the tops are level. Chill in the refrigerator for at least 2 hours.

Sprinkle the tops with the sugar. Using a chef's blow torch, broil the tops until caramelized (about 2–3 minutes). Alternatively, cook under a preheated broiler, turning the dishes, for 3–4 minutes, or until the tops are lightly caramelized all over.

Serve immediately or chill in the refrigerator for 15–20 minutes before serving.

Party Tip— Be the perfect host or hostess by providing spare winter accessories such as hats, scarves, and gloves for guests who may have forgotten theirs.

No matter how full guests may be, they will always find room for some gooey chocolate fudge pudding, especially on a cold winter evening!

chocolate fudge pudding

SERVES 4

1/3 cup soft butter
1 1/4 cups self–rising flour
1/2 cup corn syrup
3 eggs
1/4 cup unsweetened cocoa

for the chocolate
fudge sauce
3 1/2 oz/100 g semisweet
chocolate
1/2 cup condensed milk
4 tbsp heavy cream

Lightly grease a 5-cup heatproof pudding bowl.

Place the ingredients for the sponge pudding in a separate mixing bowl and beat until well combined and smooth.

Spoon the mixture into the prepared bowl and smooth the top. Cover with a disk of waxed paper and tie a pleated sheet of foil over the bowl. Steam for 1 1/2–2 hours, until the sponge is cooked and springy to the touch.

To make the sauce, break the chocolate into small pieces and place in a small pan with the condensed milk. Heat gently, stirring constantly, until the chocolate melts. Remove the pan from the heat and stir in the heavy cream.

To serve the dessert, turn it out on to a serving plate and pour over a little of the chocolate fudge sauce. Serve the remaining sauce separately.

Mix everything for this classic seasonal drink in plenty of time, heating at the last minute to be served by the glass when guests arrive.

mulled wine

SERVES 4

3 cups red wine
3 tbsp sherry
8 cloves
1 cinnamon stick
1/2 tsp ground allspice
2 tbsp clear honey
1 seedless orange,
cut into wedges
1 lemon, cut into wedges

Put the wine, sherry, cloves, cinnamon, allspice, and honey into a pan and stir together well. Warm over low heat, stirring, until just starting to simmer, but do not let it boil. Remove from the heat and pour through a strainer. Discard the cloves and cinnamon stick.

Return the wine to the pan with the orange and lemon wedges. Warm gently over very low heat, but do not let it boil. Remove from the heat, pour into heatproof glasses, and serve hot.

Party Tip— Put unopened trash bags at the bottom of your trash can under the bag in use. That way, if the bag starts to overflow, anyone who notices can remove it and find a new bag waiting to be put into action.

This is thought to have been created by Joe Sheridan in the 1940s, when he was head chef at Shannon Airport, Ireland. Sugar is essential for a good floating layer of cream.

Irish coffee

SERVES 1

6 tbsp/2 measures Irish whiskey

sugar to taste

freshly made strong black coffee

6 tbsp/2 measures heavy cream

Put the whiskey into a warmed heatproof glass with sugar to taste. Pour in the coffee and stir. When the sugar has completely dissolved, pour the cream very slowly over the back of a spoon, which is just touching the top of the coffee and the edge of the glass. Keep pouring until all the cream is added and has settled on the top.

Do not stir—drink the coffee through the cream.